THE PEAK DISTRICT

The Peak District

Landscapes Through Time

John Barnatt and Ken Smith

WIND*gather*
PRESS

The Peak District: Landscapes Through Time

© John Barnatt and Ken Smith, 2004

First published in 1997 as *The English Heritage Book of the Peak District: Landscapes Through Time* by B.T. Batsford Ltd

Published by: Windgather Press Ltd, 29 Bishop Road, Bollington, Macclesfield, Cheshire SK10 5NX

Distributed by: Central Books Ltd, 99 Wallis Road, London E9 5LN

British Library Cataloguing-in-Publication Data
A catalogue record for this book is available from the British Library

ISBN 0-9545575-5-7

Designed, typeset and originated by Carnegie Publishing Ltd, Chatsworth Road, Lancaster
Printed and bound by Cambridge University Press

Contents

Landscapes of Britain

Britain has an extraordinarily rich mix of historic landscapes. This major new series explores this diversity, through accessible and attractive books that draw on the latest archaeological and historical research. Places in Britain have a great depth of historical connections. These books show how much there is to be discovered.

Also in the series

Discovering a Welsh Landscape: Archaeology in the Clwydian Range
      Ian Brown, with photography by Mick Sharp and Jean Williamson

A Frontier Landscape: The North West in the Middle Ages
      N. J. Higham

The Humber Wetlands: The Archaeology of a Dynamic Landscape
      Robert Van de Noort

List of Illustrations

Figures

Colour plates, between pages 86 and 87

Acknowledgements

This book would not have been possible without the decades of hard work by many professional and amateur archaeologists within the Peak District and elsewhere. Discussions with many of those active today helped forge the interpretations presented here. Graeme Barker invited us to write it. Graeme also commented on a draft of the text of the first edition, as did Bill Bevan, Mathew Moran and Jim Rieuwerts. Roland Smith provided encouragement and facilitated our use of many of the photographs. The following helped with the provision of information or comments: Stewart Ainsworth, Paul Ardron, Pauline Beswick, Bill Bevan, Mark Edmonds, Daryl Garton, David Hey, Chris Heathcote, John Leach, Debbie Long, Jim Rieuwerts, Jan Stetka, Arthur Wilson and Terry Worthington. Daryl Garton gave permission for the plan of Lismore Fields to be used (Figure 5). Barbara Jones and Bill Gregory allowed the use of the data on Blackwell Hall (Figure 48).

John Barnatt would like to thank Brenda and the children David, Katy and Robert, for their forbearance and support during the long absences needed to write the text and draw the illustrations. Ken Smith would like to thank Catherine for her support and encouragement.

Gary Short drew Colour Plate 3. Alison Foster applied some of the lettering to the remaining line illustrations, all of which were drawn by John Barnatt. The information on Figure 7 and some of that on Figures 4 and 17 was taken from joint surveys undertaken by the Royal Commission on the Historical Monuments of England (now English Heritage) and the Peak Park Joint Planning Board (now the Peak District National Park Authority). Figures 4, 7, 9, 38, 43, 50, 58, 63, 67 and 73 are based on surveys undertaken by John Barnatt for the Peak District National Park Authority. The following illustrations were provided by Ray Manley, the Peak District National Park Authority's photographer: Figures 1, 8, 11, 12, 13, 19, 21, 27, 33, 42, 45, 47, 49, 51, 52, 53, 54, 55, 57, 60, 62, 64, 65, 66, 69, 70, 71, 72; Colour Plates 1, 2, 9, 10, 11, 12, 13, 16, 17. Figure 68 and the photographs used in Figure 59 are also from the Authority's collections. Sheffield City Museum provided Colour Plates 5 and 8. The following illustrations were selected from photographs donated to the Authority by the late Derrick Riley: Figure 24 and Colour Plates 7 and 14. Figure 41 is reproduced by kind permission of the Cambridge University Collection of Air Photographs. Colour Plates 4, 6 and 15 were taken by John Barnatt.

Introduction

The Peak District contains several important and distinctive archaeological landscapes. These range from large expanses of heather moorland on the eastern gritstone upland where prehistoric settlements and their fields survive because only grazing has taken place subsequently, to extensive areas covered with the now picturesque remains of what two hundred years ago were industrial wastelands. Changing farming methods over the last thousand years have shaped the walled landscapes of the limestone plateau, leaving distinctive patterns across rolling grassland. Dotted amongst these fields, on isolated patches of land, often rocky or surrounded by steep ground, vestiges of earlier settlements and a rich assortment of ancient ritual monuments have survived (Figure 1).

This book sets out to give a brief introduction to the archaeology of the Peak District from the earliest people to the modern era. While covering all periods and their interpretation, it gives emphasis to important themes which have contributed most to the shaping of the character of the region. It is organised essentially on a chronological basis, because it is easier to follow the story of people through time in this way. However, because themes are also discussed, such as medieval and post-medieval agricultural landscapes, the chronological straitjacket has occasionally been cast aside.

Traditionally many archaeological guidebooks have concentrated on specific sites and the artefacts found within them. The approach taken here is different, the emphasis being on the landscape as a whole and on how what we see today has been shaped by people in the past. This perspective allows different questions to be asked and stories to be told. Such questions include; how have societies in the past been organised at different times, and how did people chose to use and move through their landscapes? Individual sites complement the broader picture, providing detailed windows through which we can glimpse objects and structures which people have left behind. Landscape archaeology can be seen as unpeeling layers of an onion, taking away the modern to reveal what is left of the periods before. Equally important is how the patterns left from these earlier periods have been distorted by subsequent destruction. In contrast with many parts of Britain, in the Peak there has been an emphasis on pastoral farming in recent centuries and much of great antiquity has survived the plough.

FIGURE I

The Hope Valley and Kinder Scout from the air. There is a strong contrast between the high northern moorlands, where little archaeology exists except for ephemeral evidence for early hunter-gatherers, and the valleys below which are a rich palimpsest of features of all periods. The Hope Valley has been a centre of population since later prehistoric times, dominated by the Mam Tor hillfort at the head of the valley. Later, Navio Roman fort was built in the valley below, followed by the Anglo-Saxon royal manor at Hope, and the medieval castle above the fortified planned town of Castleton. Extensive medieval cultivation strips, laid out about a thousand years ago, with later closes on the slopes above, form the basis of the present field pattern in the valley. This photograph shows Mam Tor, left of centre, with Castleton and its field system below it. Peveril Castle overlooks Castleton.

FIGURE 2 (*opposite*)

The Peak District: the main places, rivers and landscape divisions. Between the limestones of the White Peak and the gritstone uplands of the Dark Peak are sheltered valleys cut into softer shale. These, together with shelves above the main gorges that cut through the limestone plateau, have been the focus for market towns and villages since medieval times. Much larger industrial centres, notably Sheyeld to the east and Manchester to the west, have grown in the coal-rich peripheries of the region. In contrast, much of the gritstone upland, cutting off the cities from the heart of the Peak, comprises bleak moorland with only occasional farms.

The Peak District: a landscape of contrasts

The Peak District lies at the southern end of the Pennines, the upland spine of northern England. It is a region with contrasting landscapes. At its heart is a limestone plateau, the White Peak. Visually this is characterised by long rolling ridges, rising from shallow upland basins cut by deep dry valleys which

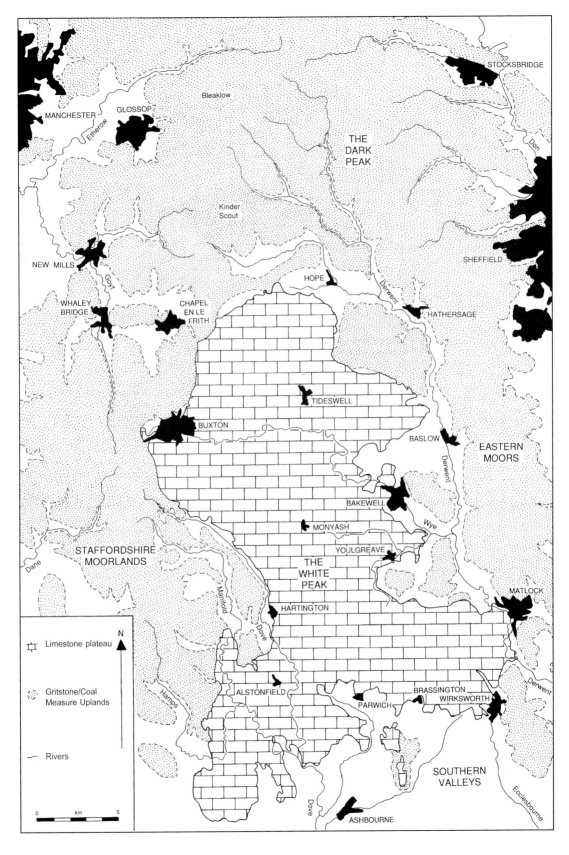

lead into precipitous-sided gorges. These shadowy gashes across the landscape drain mostly to the east and south. The highest parts of the plateau, rising in places to over 450m (1476ft) above sea level, lie predominantly to west and north. Above the main rivers there are often flat shelves, the bottoms of pre-glacial valleys later cut by the gorges as geological uplift led to radical changes in drainage characteristics. These shelves have traditionally been one of the main focal points for settlement, because of their relatively sheltered aspect and deeper soils, and the spring-lines that follow thin beds of lava which some-times occur here. Much of the rainwater that falls on the plateau percolates immediately underground, either re-emerging from caves and fissures at the edge of the plateau, or in the main rivers, whose gorges are so deep that they lie below the water table (Figure 2).

The plateau is surrounded on three sides by gritstone uplands, the Dark Peak, rising highest in the north to Kinder Scout and Bleaklow at over 600m (1968ft). These high lands are characterised by solid layers of millstone grit interleaved with shale. Where the hard grits have been cut through by erosion, prominent edges have formed. Between and above the edges are large expanses of high shelves and near-flat moortops. Today these are often poorly drained and peat-covered.

At the interface between the White and Dark Peaks the rock is mainly soft shale and this is where the main valleys of the region have formed. The River Derwent has been the main artery through the upland for millennia, providing sheltered land between contrasting upland resources. Smaller valleys to the west contain the rivers Dove and Manifold. These are more isolated, because downstream they run through long limestone gorges before reaching the lowlands to the south. Beyond the limestone plateau to the south there is a number of small valleys between low ridges which slowly drop towards the Trent valley.

Today the three landscapes just described contrast both in how they appear and how they are used. The central plateau is predominantly green fields with distinctive drystone walls of white limestone. Woodland is largely confined to the main gorges. Fields are occasionally ploughed, particularly to the east and south. The gritstone upland is mostly moorland, often heather dominated, but also commonly with coarse grasses, bracken and bilberry. In the most sheltered parts are isolated farms surrounded by fields with dark-coloured gritstone walls. At the upper margins of the farmed land many fields have reverted to moorland. The main valleys present a patchwork of ploughed and unploughed fields, sometimes with hedges rather than walls, mixed with woodland on the steeper upper slopes.

The picture would have been very different in prehistory. By the time of the first farmers, from 4000 BC to 2000 BC, the natural oscillation from glacial to interglacial had reached a warm climax, with rich diversity of temperate flora and fauna. The limestone plateau would have had a mixture of ash-dominated woodlands with broad sweeps of open pasture, naturally most common where the soils were thinner on higher land, and elsewhere where

4

cleared by people. On the gritstone upland peat had already started to form at the highest altitudes, but the majority of the landscape had open oak and birch woodland with grassy clearings, again in part enlarged by farmers. Both zones had significant areas of light fertile soils suitable for arable, as well as for pasture. The main shale valleys were naturally heavily wooded and would have been ideal for woodland grazing of cattle and pigs. While they provided good shelter for settlement, the soils were often heavier and thus more difficult to cultivate until the later introduction of iron ploughshares.

It is the reasons behind the transformation of the prehistoric landscapes to those of today which are one of the underlying themes of this volume.

Natural wealth

On the limestone plateau, the most-sheltered areas of land with the best soils are those on the shelves to either side of the main river gorges and at the gorge heads. These have probably been extensively used for agriculture and settlement since prehistory. One of the main restricting factors for settlement on the limestone is the lack of reliable water supply, except at a limited number of springs along the shelves and at the edges of the plateau. Given the restricted number of attractive options for farmers, it is likely that many of today's settlements have been occupied for millennia. Many of these would have started life as farms or small hamlets in prehistoric or Roman times, growing to villages in the medieval period (Figure 3).

The plateau has also attracted settlement because of the wealth from its rocks. While the limestone itself has traditionally been a source of lime for agriculture and building, the main resource has been the extensive mineral veins. These commonly fill faults that cut down into the rock and mine waste heaps can be followed as long lines, trending east-west across the landscape. These veins have traditionally been mined for ores of lead and to a lesser extent copper and zinc. More recently they have also been rich sources of non-metallic minerals such as calcite, fluorspar and barytes.

The main valleys beyond the plateau typically have heavy, acid soils. Outweighing these disadvantages is the shelter the valleys provide. Settlement has probably been extensive here since later prehistory if not before. The timber from woods along the valley sides, and originally throughout the valleys, has been a valuable resource.

Lower parts of the gritstone upland, particularly to the east, were extensively farmed in prehistory. Climatic decline has led to severe contraction of use, except as upland grazing, in more recent millennia. The gritstone areas to east and west have been important sources of coal.

Settlement potential

In prehistory, from 4000 BC onwards, the Peak District was one of the most important areas in Britain because of its rich, light soils. These were naturally

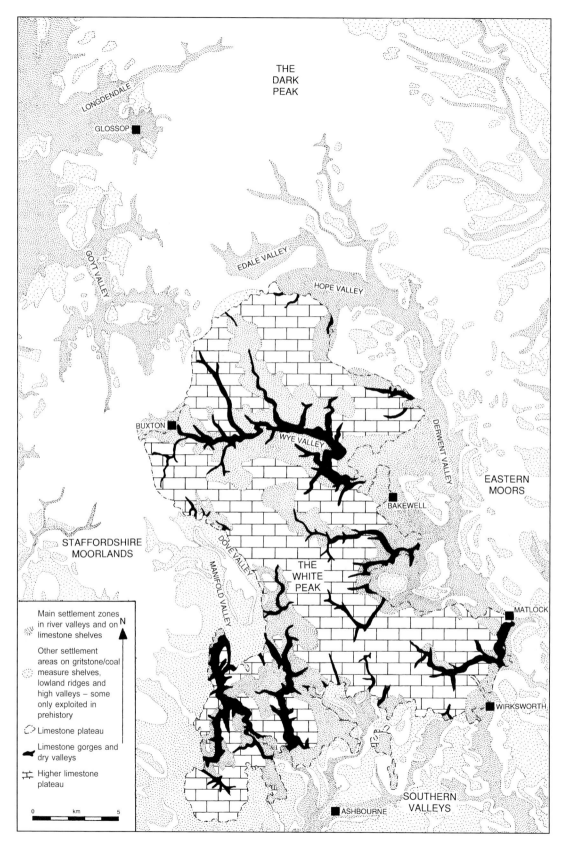

THE
DARK
PEAK

LONGDENDALE

GLOSSOP ■

GOYT VALLEY

EDALE VALLEY

HOPE VALLEY

BUXTON ■

WYE VALLEY

DERWENT VALLEY

EASTERN
MOORS

BAKEWELL ■

STAFFORDSHIRE
MOORLANDS

DOVE VALLEY

MANIFOLD VALLEY

THE
WHITE
PEAK

MATLOCK ■

Main settlement zones
in river valleys and on
limestone shelves

N

Other settlement
areas on gritstone/coal
measure shelves,
lowland ridges and
high valleys – some
only exploited in
prehistory

WIRKSWORTH ■

Limestone plateau

Limestone gorges and
dry valleys

Higher limestone
plateau

0   km   5

ASHBOURNE ■

SOUTHERN
VALLEYS

6

clear of thick forest and as a result large expanses of upland were suitable for grazing and cultivation without a great deal of effort needed to clear them. The nearest major settlement areas beyond the confines of the Peak were the gravel terraces of the Trent valley to the south, and the chalklands of the Yorkshire and Lincolnshire Wolds to the east.

With climatic decline in the centuries around 1000 BC, the agricultural productivity of the Peak District could not be sustained. Being predominantly an upland, it was more severely hit than many lowland areas. Some higher settlements and fields were eventually abandoned after several generations of farmers holding on, eventually losing the battle against lower productivity, while in other places the land continued to be worked through to today but became more marginal. High rainfall on the hills led to leaching of soils and eventually to extensive blanket bog formation.

To an extent this transformation from core area to relative agricultural back-water was offset on the limestone plateau by the wealth obtained from its lead mines throughout most of the historic period. In medieval and post-medieval times coal mines to east and west have also been worked. However, richer coal and iron mines in the foothills beyond the Peak District, where there have been major transformations over the last 500 years, led to the industrial landscapes of Sheffield and Manchester.

Past archaeological research

Digging into archaeological sites in the region may have begun as early as the Roman period, as several prehistoric burial chambers, for example at Minninglow between Parwich and Elton, seem to have been opened at this time. However, it was only from the second half of the eighteenth century that local antiquarians started recording what they found. One of the most famous of these was Thomas Bateman. He and his associate, Samuel Carrington, dug hundreds of burial mounds in the Peak District in the 1840s and 1850s. While dug with unholy haste by comparison with today's exacting methods, Bateman set new standards for his day. With his death the number of recorded excavations in the region dropped off markedly; most of the known barrows had been opened!

Until the second half of the twentieth century most investigations continued to be at prehistoric ritual monuments. It is only in recent decades that the balance has begun to be redressed, with the excavation of settlements and their fields, and at defensive and industrial sites. However, being upland and mostly

FIGURE 3 (*opposite*)
The Peak District: its topography and traditional areas of settlement. The region is one of great topographical contrasts. Parts of the Dark Peak are unsuitable for anything but upland grazing from scattered hill farms. At the other extreme, on the limestone plateau, on gritstone shelves and in the main valleys, areas can be identified which have traditionally been foci for settlement since prehistory. Gorges and dry valleys cutting the limestone plateau are precipitously steep, but the higher parts of the plateau have always been valuable grazing land.

within a National Park, the region has escaped much of the modern development seen elsewhere. Nationally, in recent decades, funds have been directed towards excavation ahead of development. Relatively few sites have been dug in the Peak District as a result. The majority of excavations that have occurred have been at sites of prehistoric and Roman date, with few at medieval or later sites. This imbalance is offset by ongoing extensive survey of unexcavated archaeological features of all periods in the last three decades, often at a landscape scale. The current number of known 'sites' in the region is well over 10,000 and significant numbers of new ones are discovered every year. In recent years there has been a growing realisation that all features in the landscape created by people, including houses, outbuildings, field boundaries, field kilns, routeways and industrial remains, often have a long history and have great value. In a sense, 'sites' are only hotspots within a broader landscape of equal if not greater importance.

The present landscape: its historic character and archaeological features

This book draws on the data from all these disparate research programmes, excavations and surveys, and charts the thousands of years of human use of the Peak District landscapes they inhabited. While the hills and valleys of the Peak are the result of geological processes, the whole of this landscape, including its plants and animals, has been shaped by people and is imbued with historic character. This rich tapestry which changes from place to place, our legacy from past generations, can be visited and more fully appreciated and enjoyed once you learn to read it.

Much of the Peak District landscape has a palimpsest of archaeological features of all periods, with traces of earlier features being identified amongst the greater detail of the currently-used landscape, with its settlements, fields and moors, much of which has been slowly shaped over the last two thousand years. One of its attractions is finding industrial and agricultural features built in recent centuries cheek by jowl with ruined structures built millennia ago. On the gritstone upland, whole ancient landscapes are still discernible because of the lack of later intensive agriculture. Being an upland, the region has not suffered as much from the devastations of modern mechanised farming. Features of great antiquity are sometimes still in use today, as part of a living landscape with farming roots going back into the distant past (Figure 4).

FIGURE 4 (*opposite*)
Gardom's Edge: a multi-period archaeological landscape. This area of gritstone shelf, high above Baslow in the Derwent valley below, illustrates the complexity of the archaeological remains sometimes found in the Peak District. The earliest site is the large ritual enclosure on the crest of the shelf, built in the Neolithic at about 3000 BC. On the slopes north and east of this are extensive prehistoric field boundaries and clearance cairns, together with house sites and ceremonial monuments, probably first laid out around 2000 BC. These survive in an area mainly used in subsequent centuries for rough grazing. In contrast, large parts of the better-aspected south-facing slopes of Gardom's Edge have been farmed more recently, perhaps even continuously since prehistory. There are also important industrial remains, including early coal mines, and quarries where millstones were made, used throughout Britain from late medieval times onwards.

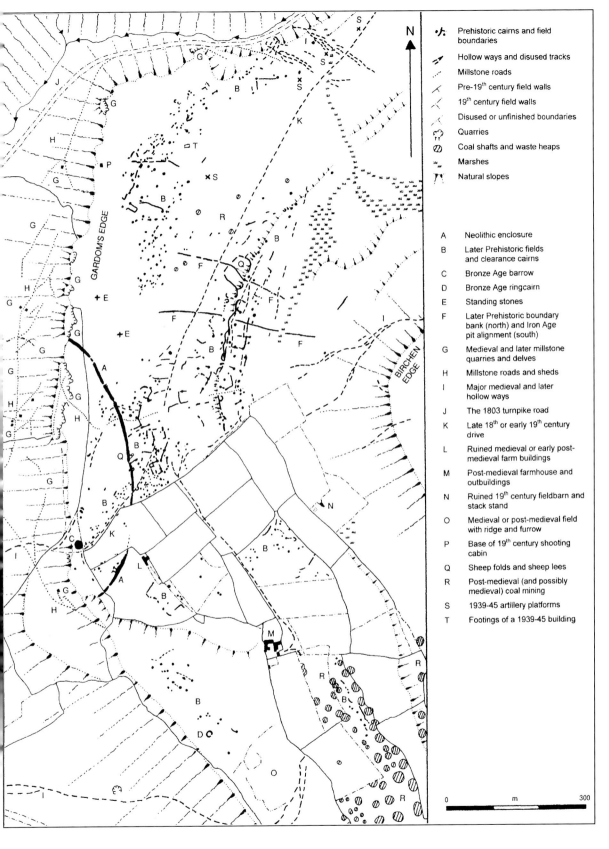

Symbol	Description
	Prehistoric cairns and field boundaries
	Hollow ways and disused tracks
	Millstone roads
	Pre-19th century field walls
	19th century field walls
	Disused or unfinished boundaries
	Quarries
	Coal shafts and waste heaps
	Marshes
	Natural slopes

A Neolithic enclosure

B Later Prehistoric fields and clearance cairns

C Bronze Age barrow

D Bronze Age ringcairn

E Standing stones

F Later Prehistoric boundary bank (north) and Iron Age pit alignment (south)

G Medieval and later millstone quarries and delves

H Millstone roads and sheds

I Major medieval and later hollow ways

J The 1803 turnpike road

K Late 18th or early 19th century drive

L Ruined medieval or early post-medieval farm buildings

M Post-medieval farmhouse and outbuildings

N Ruined 19th century fieldbarn and stack stand

O Medieval or post-medieval field with ridge and furrow

P Base of 19th century shooting cabin

Q Sheep folds and sheep lees

R Post-medieval (and possibly medieval) coal mining

S 1939-45 artillery platforms

T Footings of a 1939-45 building

GARDOM'S EDGE

BIRCHEN EDGE

0   m   300

Exploiting the Natural Landscape: Caves and Upland Camps

....

Hunter or hunted: the earliest gatherer-hunters

Humans have probably visited and exploited the Peak District over at least the last 500,000 years. The earliest times are known by archaeologists as the Palaeolithic and end with the retreat of the most recent ice sheets that covered Britain some 10,000 years ago. It was a time of climatic fluctuations, with cold glacial periods alternating with warm interglacials. Some of these interglacial periods, such as that continuing to the present day, lasted tens of thousands of years. Some reached semi-tropical conditions at their heights with the region being grazed by animals such as elephant, rhinoceros and hippopotamus. At the other extreme, and more commonly, the climate was much colder than today. When not actually ice-covered, the region would have been tundra, with large herds of mammals such as reindeer entering it in summer from the surrounding lowlands.

Throughout the Palaeolithic, early humans were gatherer-hunters. Their small numbers and mobile lifestyle has left little in the archaeological record except worked flints, animal bone tools and the bones of the animals they had eaten. Perishable materials such as wood and skins have not survived. They collected roots, tubers, leaves, fruits, nuts and berries and they also hunted animals for food and for raw materials like bone, antler and hides. Subsequent erosion of the landscape and redeposition of soils over ten thousand years means that archaeological evidence for this period in the Peak District only survives in exceptional circumstances, such as in caves. As a result it is not clear if humans normally lived in the open and only visited caves for ritual activities, if they used them only in extreme weather conditions, or if they preferred the relative security and shelter of caves. Where animal and human bones have been found together in caves elsewhere, it seems that sometimes humans themselves were the prey, their remains brought to the caves by other predatory animals.

Over ten caves in the Peak District have produced small amounts of Palaeolithic material, including Thors Fissure Cave, Elder Bush Cave, and Ossum's Cave, all in the Manifold valley. These were in use late in the glacial era during relatively cold conditions. At Elder Bush Cave reindeer meat had been stored in a stone boxlike structure. None of the Peak District caves contain large amounts of material when compared with those outside the region a short distance to the east at Creswell Crags, near Bolsover. The caves there are exceptional and are one of the most important Palaeolithic sites in western Europe.

Forest and fire: the post-glacial seasonal round

The present warm interglacial started a little over 10,000 years ago and for about the first 5000 of those years people continued to subsist as gatherer-hunters in the Peak District. However, archaeologically, there is a contrast with what went before. Artefacts are found in soils throughout the region while finds from caves are few. The archaeological evidence largely comprises stone tools and production waste. The most diagnostic of these artefacts are microliths, small carefully-shaped points made from flint and chert. Normally several of these points and barbs would have been fixed together into wooden shafts to make composite artefacts such as arrows for hunting. Other common tools were scrapers and simple knives. Objects of wood, bone and hide again have rarely survived.

Stone tools are found throughout the Peak District, wherever soils are being disturbed by human or natural agencies like ploughing or erosion. Where soils are not often disturbed, such as the eastern and western gritstone moorlands, evidence for past human activity may well be significantly under-represented. Significantly, artefacts of this period, known as the Mesolithic, are relatively common where peat is eroding on the high moorlands of the northern Dark Peak, while flintwork from later periods is not. This reflects this area's suitability for hunting but not for agriculture. Thus, in this area, hunting camps can be studied without the problems of later flintwork being mixed with the recovered material.

Gatherer-hunters today do not lead a haphazard, catch-as-catch-can existence. Usually they have a carefully planned seasonal round, moving through a familiar territory, following traditional routes to make the best use of resources as they become available through the year. In the Peak District it is easy to imagine bands moving between winter and summer from the forested lowlands to either side of the Pennines up onto the more open limestone and gritstone uplands.

The Mesolithic is divided by archaeologists into Earlier and Later on the basis of different tool types. For example, microliths become smaller in the Later Mesolithic, reflecting changes in the environment, from predominantly open landscape to one that was largely wooded. Types of game changed, from large easily-hunted herds of reindeer and bison, to small, scattered herds of red deer, much more difficult to hunt within the forest.

The gradual increase in post-glacial sea level around Britain, caused by the melting of the glacial ice-caps, flooded extensive coastal plains rich in wildlife and separated Britain from the rest of continental Europe about 6000 BC. In response to these changes, people were forced to change exploitation strategies and the seasonal round probably became more geographically restricted. In the Peak District there was a change from using flint from the Yorkshire and Lincolnshire Wolds in the Earlier Mesolithic to the use later of chert found locally on the limestone plateau. This suggests that the traditional sources of raw material were not available to the people using the Peak District as they no longer travelled as far east as previously.

As a response to the stresses placed on Later Mesolithic gatherer-hunter bands, people appear, for the first time, to have made a radical impact on the natural environment. Changes in fossil pollen preserved in the peat, together with fragments of charcoal here, show that small clearings were burnt in the forest, to focus game on the rich new growth that resulted. Hunting was thus transformed, with more game at predictable locations. However, this was not a sustainable strategy in uplands such as the Dark Peak where there is relatively high rainfall. Once the tree cover was broken the nutrients in the soil were washed down the profile and eventually a hard, impermeable iron-rich layer formed. In the end the ground became waterlogged and peat formation started. Much of the deep blanket bogs of the high Dark Peak cover tree stumps dating to the Later Mesolithic and Earlier Neolithic. Such transformed areas supported less game and new clearings were necessary, resulting in large areas of trees eventually being removed. This downward spiral, that started in the Mesolithic, was probably one of the significant factors in the adoption of farming by the local hunter-gatherers at the beginning of the Neolithic, about 4000 BC. Intensification as a response to environmental and social stresses continues to this day.

CHAPTER TWO

Open Pastures and Enclosed Fields: The Landscapes of the First Farmers

The first farmers: summer pastures and winter retreats

The most common evidence for the Peak District's first farmers is widespread scatters of stone tools and production waste, the small pieces of flint broken off during the manufacture or renewal of those tools. These have been found across the landscape, wherever lost or discarded. Neolithic artefacts, dating from the period *c.*4000 BC–2000 BC, commonly comprise knives, scrapers, borers and arrowheads made of flint and chert. Dwellings, made of perishable materials, have not been found, with notable exceptions at Buxton described below. Impressive ritual monuments built by these people are discussed in Chapter 3.

Although it is clear Neolithic farmers were present in the Peak District in some numbers, reconstructing details of their activities is difficult. Stone tools were used in the Neolithic, as well as earlier in the Mesolithic and later in the Bronze Age. Scatters of these tools and production waste are found, mainly in today's ploughed fields, over large areas in overlapping patches of different densities. However, systematic collection and appropriate analysis of flint material in the Peak District is still in its infancy. One problem is that diagnostic arrowheads have previously been used to date scatters into which they may have been accidentally introduced; arrowheads are the one artefact type that has a high chance of being lost well away from habitation during hunting. Another problem is that in the past different collectors have worked different areas to different standards. There are also significant differences in the amounts of land ploughed across the Peak District. At the same time, large areas of the gritstone are open moorland where flints have only been found occasionally, usually after intense fires have removed the peat cover and led to erosion of the soils beneath.

All these factors have led to biases in the available data and to interpretations that can be questioned. For example, it has traditionally been argued that the main focus of Neolithic activity in the Peak District was the limestone plateau. However, systematic pilot work carried out in the 1980s, followed by large-scale ongoing collection since the mid-1990s, is demonstrating that Neolithic and Bronze Age flint-scatters are relatively common across the three landscape zones tested; the limestone plateau, the Wye and Derwent valleys and the eastern gritstone uplands.

More dramatic confirmation that Neolithic activity was not confined to the limestone plateau came in the late 1980s from excavations on clayland at Lismore Fields, on the west side of Buxton, one of the most important Neolithic settlements found so far in Britain. Very unusually in a British context there was evidence of timber buildings. Other excavations in the Peak District, at flint scatters at Mount Pleasant and Aleck Low, in the heart of the limestone plateau south of Arbor Low, found only ephemeral evidence for structures. At Mount Pleasant this consisted of small and shallow rectangular hollows, perhaps the site of temporary structures. In contrast, the buildings at Lismore Fields were well-built timber houses with central hearths. The careful

FIGURE 5

The Neolithic settlement at Lismore Fields, Buxton. One of the most important aspects of the excavated portion of this settlement are the rectangular buildings. These were of similar design to each other, built of timber and defined today by postholes along the lines of outer walls and internal divisions. Building 1 was twice the size of the other. However, it may be that it starting life identical to building 2, but then had a later structure of similar shape and size added to one end, either as an enlargement to, or a replacement of, the earlier house. Associated with these buildings were several pits. There were also two lines of large free-standing posts, at right angles to each other. A series of nine small circular structures, defined by either closely spaced postholes or continuous slots, are of unknown date and uncertain function. The settlement has been dated by a series of radiocarbon dates to the centuries around 3500 BC. The site was also occupied at an earlier date, evidenced by knapping scatters of Mesolithic flintwork. However, continuous use of the site from one period to the other cannot be demonstrated.

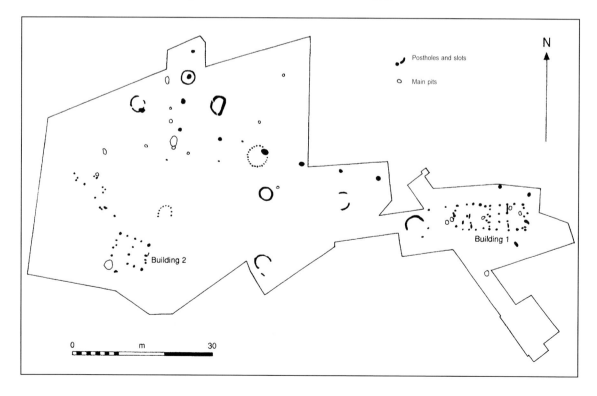

nature of their construction and the presence of associated structures suggest a settlement designed to be used over a long period. Timber buildings, when kept warm and dry, can be used for several hundred years. The people who lived at Lismore Fields certainly used and discarded flint and chert tools, as well as polished stone axes and plain but well-made pottery. Careful excavation revealed charred emmer wheat, flax seeds, hazelnuts and the fruits and seeds of crab apples. Other evidence of their way of life has not survived the passage of time. For example, wooden artefacts and discarded animal bones must have been plentiful but were not found (Figure 5).

The site itself was located on the low-lying clayland of the upper Wye valley basin between the limestone plateau to the south and the gritstone uplands to the north. It was therefore easy for people to exploit the three landscape zones with their contrasting topographies and their different and often complementary resources. People in the Peak District as a whole may well have had similar opportunities. The main valleys such as that of the Derwent or that of the upper Wye basin around Buxton, while heavily wooded, would have provided the best shelter and thus have been ideally suitable for overwintering. They would also have been an important source of fish, fruit and fowl. In contrast, the limestone plateau and eastern gritstone uplands contained large areas nearer the tree line, that may have been only intermittently wooded or at least were more easily cleared than the valleys. These would have been ideal for summer grazing. Both limestone and gritstone zones contain areas of light fertile soils suitable for tillage by spade, hoe or ard (the precursor to the plough). The northern and western gritstone uplands were significantly higher and may have mainly been used for hunting. Animal bones survived badly at Lismore Fields because of the acidity of the clay soils. It is therefore not possible at present to build up a picture of what domestic stock were kept at this site or to what use they were put, or what wild animals were hunted.

One type of Neolithic artefact suggests the way people were beginning to change the landscape. Polished axes were sometimes made of flint, but more commonly of various hard igneous rocks from sources such as Cumbria and North Wales, acquired by people in the Peak District over such long distances by trade or exchange. Several hundred have been found in the Peak District, with one from as far away as Northern Ireland. Some of the larger and more carefully made examples of polished axes are in pristine condition suggesting they were symbolic objects, used exclusively in ceremonies or as status symbols. However, the majority were practical tools for felling trees or perhaps for use as hoes for cultivation.

Long term, these two activities would have had an impact on the landscape. Timber was needed for construction of buildings and other structures and for many artefacts, such as containers and handles for tools and weapons. Evidence from elsewhere in Britain suggests that even at this early date, people were managing woodlands to get the types of timber that they required. Such activities as coppicing would have been easy tasks to undertake with the available stone technology. Agriculture would have made its own mark on the landscape. Preference was probably given to cultivation in sheltered locations with easily-worked soils and this may have influenced the choice of site for habitation, chosen for easy access and management of the growing crops, and to provide protection from wild and domestic animals. Woodland would have been cleared to create both arable plots and to enlarge grazing pastures and the appearance of the landscape began to change as a result. Such processes have culminated in the agricultural landscapes found in the Peak District today.

Throughout much of the Neolithic it may be that the first farmers had a seasonal round similar to their gatherer-hunter forebears. They were probably predominantly pastoralists, keeping cattle, sheep and pigs, moving round the limestone plateau and other uplands in summer and retreating to lower ground in winter. Arable cultivation may have been confined to small garden plots, growing cereals and possibly peas and beans on the sheltered lower limestone and gritstone shelves. Traditional claims to the most competed-over seasonal pastures, on the limestone plateau, were reinforced by the building of monuments dedicated to the ancestors.

That this way of life was successful is demonstrated by the picture at the end of the Neolithic, around 2000 BC. Artefacts and monuments made around this time are common, indicating a population that had grown significantly. As a result their lifestyle was gradually becoming more place-orientated as traditional claims on land became fixed. Sustainable settlements spread from the sheltered valleys into the more favourable areas of the limestone plateau and gritstone uplands suitable for mixed farming.

Enclosing the landscape: later prehistoric farms

The eastern gritstone upland landscape contains exceptional evidence for prehistoric farming. The visible archaeology comprises many small clearance cairns, intermittent stretches of low stony or earthen banks at the edges of fields and yards, and slight terraced platforms marking the sites of circular houses. These features are frequently masked by moorland vegetation and are often found with the feet rather than the eye. It is when maps are made of their relation one to another that their true importance emerges, large areas of cleared land and defined fields often becoming clear. Associated with many of the clusters of fields and cairnfields is the occasional small ritual monument,

FIGURE 6 (*opposite*)
Later prehistoric settlement on the Eastern Moors of the Peak District. This map shows the wide extent of surviving later prehistoric settlement and fields on the gritstone uplands flanking the Derwent Valley. These are most frequent on the high shelves overlooking the Derwent valley, where the altitude is low enough for viable mixed farming but high enough to have escaped destruction by later farmers. Although the surviving remains are frequent, examination of the distribution of more modern fields across the region, which are normally in similar but better aspected locations to their earlier counterparts, suggests the prehistoric settlements were once significantly more extensive than is obvious today. This is particularly true towards the south, while to the north the moors tend to become higher and were less suitable for farming even in prehistory. At the height of prehistoric exploitation there may well have been many farms on this upland, supporting a population in the low thousands; in strong contrast to the few scattered farms of today.

16

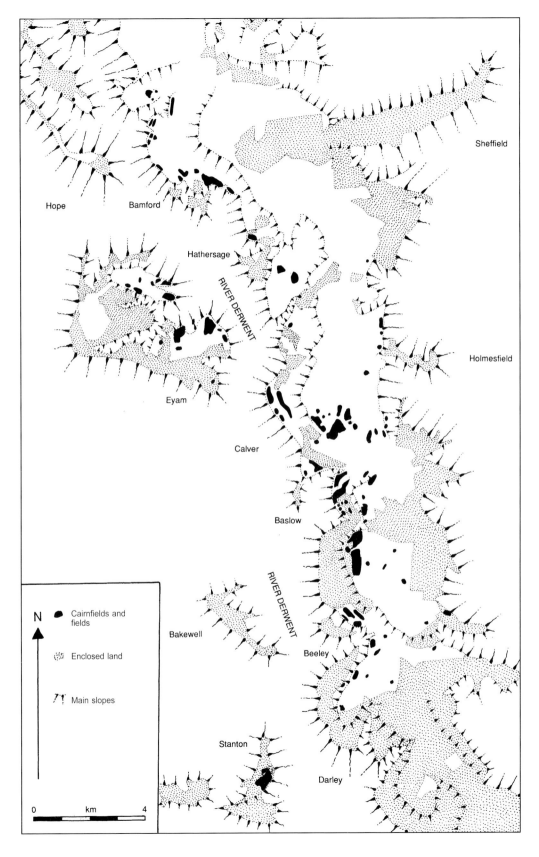

N

● Cairnfields and fields

⠿ Enclosed land

↗↑ Main slopes

Sheffield

Hope

Bamford

Hathersage

RIVER DERWENT

Holmesfield

Eyam

Calver

Baslow

Bakewell

RIVER DERWENT

Beeley

Stanton

Darley

0   km   4

usually the barrows and stone circles of Bronze Age date discussed in Chapter 3 (Figure 6).

The groups of fields and clearance cairns, of which there are over seventy, are found in specific predictable locations along the eastern upland. Topographically this gritstone upland is similar throughout its length. The main scarp rises about 150m (490ft) from the Derwent below. Above this there is a broad main shelf and above that is a second scarp, often about 50m (165ft) high, with upper moors beyond. In places the upper scarp is broken by streams and these have flanking shelves. It is the main shelf and upper shelves where the prehistoric fields are found, mostly at an altitude of between 250m (820ft) and 350m (1150ft). These locations had light sandy soils in prehistory, ideally suitable for cultivation by early farmers. In contrast, much of the upland elsewhere was covered by heavy clays. The main exception was the crest of the upper scarp which again had sandy soils. These areas were not used for agriculture, even where not too high, because more favourable locations were available locally on the shelves below.

Today much of the upland is covered in thin peaty soils and is bleak and inhospitable heather moorland, which begs the question, why did prehistoric people want to live and farm here? The answer is that things have changed. The climate was somewhat warmer and dryer, when local communities started cultivating these areas. Soil deterioration was sparked off later by a worsening of the climate and by people trying to maintain the same farming strategy under changed conditions. At the outset of farming the vegetation of the upland comprised a mixture of grassland and open woodlands. The area was attractive because clearance was relatively easy here compared with the densely wooded valleys below.

As with many parts of upland Britain, the surviving evidence for early farming is found on the best available land just below the altitude threshold of viable prehistoric agriculture. Lower down surface evidence for prehistoric farming has been destroyed subsequently by later agriculture over the last two millennia. On the eastern gritstone upland the upper limit of later destruction is mostly nineteenth century in date, where there are farmsteads within walled fields. The best-aspected lower shelves may have been farmed continuously since prehistory, much of the historic evidence having been masked, in the same way that the prehistoric evidence has been, by the last wave of upward advance. In exceptional instances, as on Gardom's Edge, east of Baslow (see Figure 4), fragmentary remains of all periods are found at the edges of stony land within post-medieval fields. The nineteenth-century destruction would have been much greater, with most or all of the prehistoric remains removed, if it was not for the use of the eastern moorlands by powerful landowners for grouse shooting, who thus prevented them being 'improved' by farmers. Although the prehistoric fields on the eastern moors are some of the best in Britain, the predictability of the topography allows it to be estimated that less than half of these field clusters survives, the rest having disappeared under later enclosure.

It used to be thought that, on the eastern moors, agricultural areas with fields could be identified, distinct from cemetery areas with cairns and monuments. Generally this is not true. The groups of fields and cairns on Big Moor, north-east of Baslow, are a good example that demonstrate why not, both here and for the region as a whole. It was suggested that the land west of Bar Brook was used for habitation and agriculture and that to the east was used exclusively for rituals and burial. Careful comparison of the two zones shows that there is no basis for this distinction. There are similar numbers of small cairns on either side of the stream and they have the same range of sizes. There are also similar numbers of stone circles and large barrows in both zones. The only real distinction is the presence of visible field boundaries west of Bar Brook but not to the east. The linear banks that define the fields west of Bar Brook are of two contrasting types, neither of which are likely to be collapsed boundaries in themselves. The stony ones are short and discontinuous, and are more likely to be clearance heaps up against continuous boundaries that can no longer be seen. The other main type comprises continuous earthen banks. Excavation on Big Moor demonstrated that there were no adjacent ditches to provide material with which to build them, and there was no identifiable buried turfline or topsoil underneath them. This suggests that the banks probably mark the sites of hedges or fences which acted as wind traps for soil being blown about. Thus, while the surface of tilled fields was being eroded slightly, the banks were slowly being formed. The continuous earthen boundaries at Big Moor and other groups of fields are on the exposed tops of shelves, where wind transportation is likely to have been greatest. It is against such hedges or fences that discontinuous linear clearance would also have accumulated (Figure 7).

The dichotomy between areas with and without boundaries is best explained by varying physical conditions and different agricultural histories. Sites with good boundary definition are likely to have been used more intensively over short periods or more extensively over longer periods of time than those without, giving the opportunities for banks to form in exposed locations and for clearance to accumulate at field edges. Several further factors influence this process, including degree of stoniness; amount of shelter; the extent to which fields were tilled rather than used for pasture; and the degree of late use at a time when soils were deteriorating and being lost.

To explain all small cairns as clearance heaps is simplistic. While it may well be that this was the primary function of the vast majority of small cairns, a proportion of these apparently simple heaps also contains ritual deposits and human burials. It may well be that the placing of these within fields, and the similar location of ritual monuments such as barrows and stone circles, had great symbolic significance, perhaps concerned with regeneration and fertility of the soil and the well-being of the community. This is borne out at recent excavations at Sir William Hill above Eyam, where a simple clearance heap at the top of the small cairnfield here was later enlarged at around 2000 BC over three ritual pits. These contained purposefully-placed flint scrapers, sherds of

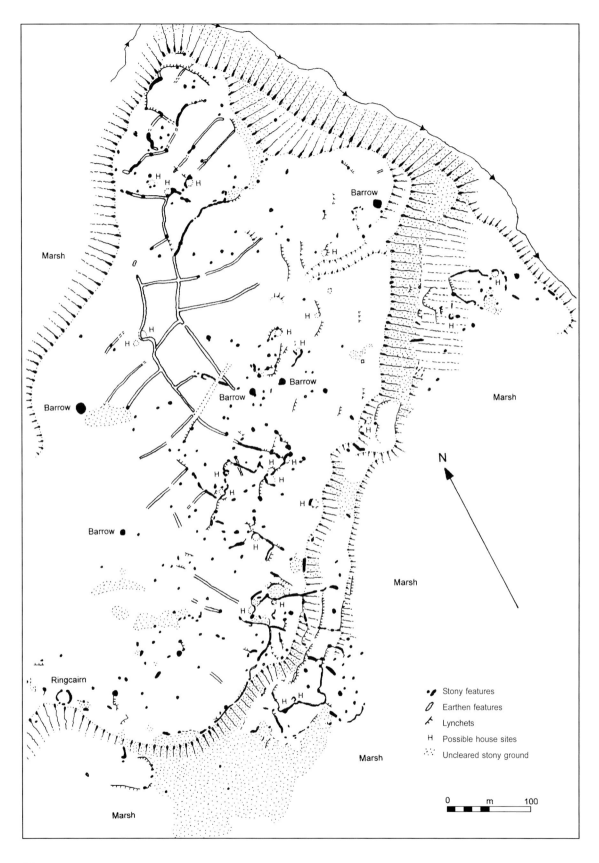

Marsh

Marsh

Barrow

Marsh

Barrow

Barrow
Barrow

N

Barrow

Marsh

Ringcairn

Marsh

	Stony features
	Earthen features
	Lynchets
H	Possible house sites
	Uncleared stony ground

0   m   100

Marsh

Beaker pottery, a chert rubber, a saddle quern, a small token deposit of cremated bone and what was probably domestic debris. These items hint at complex symbolic gestures that linked everyday life with the beliefs of the people who worked the land. At extensive recent excavations above Gardom's Edge near Baslow, most of the small cairns investigated proved to be simple heaps of stone with no evidence of ritual deposition. However, one, placed between two of the main areas of fields, covered what appeared to be a grave pit, the bones long since decomposed. This cairn was later enlarged and surrounded by a kerb of carefully-placed stones. Two other cairns with crude kerbs had potsherds placed immediately outside them.

In only three cairnfields can a case be made that they were perhaps primarily funerary rather than agricultural; these are discussed further in Chapter 3.

Prehistoric houses within the fields were normally built of timber, with no stone footings. They are no longer visible as surface remains. However, in a proportion of cases, their sites are known. Sometimes this is from the size of defined plots. Where smaller than usual it is likely these were yards or gardens associated with houses whose sites cannot now be seen. In some instances circular houses were abutted by enclosure banks, leaving distinctive arcs of bank. On slopes, house sites can be seen as levelled circular platforms. The recent excavations at Gardom's Edge have confirmed these sites contain houses. Two smaller circular houses had large door posts and the walls were built of hurdlework. At one of these there was the cremation of a child in a pit within the house, placed under a timber structure which can be interpreted as a house shrine. When this house was abandoned its entrance was blocked by a stone bank upon which were placed inverted saddle querns, a symbolic act closing down its life. A third house was large and had a porch; it contained several pits, including one with an inverted saddle quern. There is evidence for several phases of use, some perhaps after the timber house had gone but its site was still respected. Surrounding stone banks were built, ending at large boulders placed over the porch postholes. There was a subsequent narrowing of the entrance which was then paved (Figure 8).

It used to be thought that the prehistoric fields of the eastern moors represented short and perhaps seasonal episodes of cultivation that were abandoned as soils rapidly became exhausted. As they are normally associated with Earlier

FIGURE 7 (*opposite*)

The central later prehistoric fields on Big Moor, Baslow. This prehistoric area of fields is typical in many ways of this type of site in the Peak District, although it is more extensive than most and has better defined field boundaries than some. Visible boundaries occur in two forms. Short stony features are linear clearance against field edges, while earthen banks exist on the shelf top, where soil has blown from the fields and been trapped by hedges to form low banks. Below the shelf to the east there are two main sheltered areas where houses are found surrounded by small yards and garden-plots. The one to the south is known as Swine Sty and has been partially excavated. Further concentrations of buildings on the shelf above suggest that shelter was not an essential factor in house location. However, it is far from clear if all these areas were occupied at any one time, or whether farm sites migrated. The layout of the fields is complex, giving the impression that they were built and used over a long period, developing in aggregate fashion, new boundaries adding to and modifying what was already there. The relationship of fields to house-groups suggests that at its height between two and four farms exploited the fields here.

The excavated building at Swine Sty, Big Moor, Baslow. This building within a small enclosing stone-banked enclosure at the southern end of the Big Moor field system was excavated in the 1960s. The visible circular feature is a rare stone-footed building. It has a single entrance; the superstructure was built of timber, probably comprising a conical roof that was either thatched or covered in turves. This structure was preceded by a timber building without stone footings, only the postholes of which were found. It was abutted on one side by the enclosure bank, which curves in an arc at this point. This building was nearly twice the diameter of its successor and may well be a typical dwelling. In contrast, the later building is particularly small and may be a shepherd's shelter, built after much of the settlement had been abandoned. The Swine Sty excavations not only produced artefacts typical of a domestic and farming settlement, but showed that it was the site of a cottage industry manufacturing polished shale rings, some large enough to be bracelets, others of more uncertain purpose.

Bronze Age ritual monuments dateable to *c.* 2000 BC–1500 BC, it was assumed the farming all dated to this restricted horizon. As more evidence has accumulated, a strong case can be made that settlement was permanent and that farming took place for something like 2000 years. The recent excavations at Sir William Hill have confirmed for the first time the presence of early clearance, dated to before *c.* 2000 BC. In favourable locations, as on Gardom's Edge, the farming probably continued well into the Iron Age, while at Stoke Flat above Curbar recent radiocarbon dating of environmental samples suggests farming did not cease until the late Iron Age or early Roman period. Several of the clusters of fields contain evidence of long periods of use, with features overlapping each other and with evidence for changes of field layout. At Eaglestone Flat, above Baslow, excavation showed that what looked to be a simple linear clearance feature was complex and had an associated cremation cemetery (see Chapter 3). Radiocarbon dates show this site was added to over several hundred years. Swine Sty, on Big Moor, for many years the only excavated settlement, was originally interpreted as being Earlier Bronze Age. However, our current knowledge of domestic artefacts suggests some of the flintwork may be Later Neolithic (*c.*3000–2000 BC), while the pottery includes Later Bronze Age and Earlier Iron Age forms (*c.*1500–500 BC), similar to that found at the settlement within the Mam Tor hillfort. The excavated houses at Gardom's Edge also had large quantities of similar late pottery, although some earlier pottery and other artefacts of later Neolithic and Earlier Bronze Age date were found in the sheltered northern part of the extensive area of fields here (Figure 9).

All this evidence suggests that settlement may have started in the Later Neolithic, and given the common association with ritual monuments, was perhaps at a peak in about 2000 BC–1500 BC. However, it is also likely that many of the groups of fields continued in use long after the construction of distinctive monuments had gone out of fashion. Some of the more favourable sites with well-defined boundaries continued to be farmed until around the time the Romans arrived. These may well have been finally abandoned after farmers had fought a long battle with deteriorating soils, brought on by the climatic deterioration earlier in the millennium, no doubt reluctant to give up family land that had been inhabited for many generations. A few settlements, in locations where farms exist today, may have continued in use into the Roman period and beyond.

In the Neolithic initial exploitation of the eastern gritstone upland may have started as seasonal grazing. In the Bronze Age the farms, surrounded by their hedged fields, probably practised mixed farming on a more sustained and perhaps year-round basis. Pollen analysis has certainly established that cereals were grown, whereas animal bones do not survive because of the acid soils. However, it seems likely that animals were an important part of the economy, as is usually the case in uplands. Sheep and cattle may well have grazed both in the fields and in the extensive unenclosed areas beyond. While small-scale cultivation probably took place to cater for each farm's needs, in any given year most fields were probably grass, perhaps used as hay meadows in the summer, while the stock were grazed in the open pastures beyond. In the winter the animals were perhaps brought into the fields and their manure would have helped maintain soil fertility. It was the flocks of sheep and herds of cattle which would have provided the successful farmer with a source of surplus which allowed exchange for other goods, such as flint and at later date metal tools, necessary to maintaining a comfortable life.

The sites of buildings can be found singly or in small clusters in most areas of fields. This suggests that the land was cultivated from scattered farms

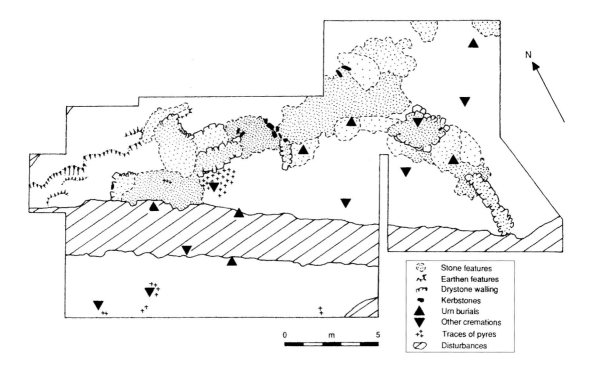

🝆	Stone features
⅄	Earthen features
⌒	Drystone walling
🝆	Kerbstones
▲	Urn burials
▼	Other cremations
⁺⁺	Traces of pyres
⬭	Disturbances

0   m   5

FIGURE 9

The cairns, walls and cremation cemetery at Eaglestone Flat. Excavation of this site, high on the gritstone upland above Baslow, shows how complex the prehistoric features amongst the fields can be upon excavation. The site was discovered after a large open drain was dug through it. At least eight phases of prehistoric activity can be identified, taking place over several hundreds of years in the Bronze Age. The abutting features included simple clearance heaps and stone spreads, retained stone platforms and unusual faced walls that were only ever one or two courses high, probably with low earthen banks above. These features were at one edge of an island of stony ground within land cultivated in prehistory. In, under and around the stone features were buried 15 human cremations. Some were placed in pots within pits in the ground. In one case the pot was inverted on a large slab within a purpose-built cairn of slabs leant against it. These pot burials may well have been imported from cremation pyres elsewhere on the eastern moors. Other burials at Eaglestone Flat were found in simple pits in the ground, all of which had burnt sides. These deposits were made immediately after cremation rites took place on site. Evidence for several pyres was found, including one intact example. Funerary goods that survived the pyres were varied, including stone tools, a perforated antler plate and faience beads. Particularly poignant was a bone whistle placed at the centre of a child cremation within a small urn. Another cremation urn had had a previous use and contained what may be fish oil mixed with red ochre.

located within the fields, each probably occupied by an extended family or kin group. The fact that each cluster of fields is separated from those of farming neighbours by unenclosed land, and has its own ritual monuments, suggests that every small farming community had its own identity, with its own defined home territory. This included both fields and upland grazing, as well as the ritual monuments, and thus each local community had everything necessary for their everyday practical and spiritual well-being. These farmers were no doubt at the same time part of a wider community, with close family and social links with neighbours and people further afield.

CHAPTER THREE

Sacred Landscapes: Monuments for the Living and the Dead

....

The sacred and the profane: the role of monuments

The distinction drawn between the sacred and profane, discussing ritual monuments separate to settlement and fields, is one of convenience. However, both archaeological monuments in Britain and anthropological research in the third world show that it is one that reflects modern attitudes and probably not those of the people who built the monuments. It may be that the builders made little distinction between the spiritual and the practical. All places and things may have been imbued with spirit and everyday activities seen as having ritual aspects. Equally, ritual sites were practical places from the builders' perspective, where activities took place that helped make sense of the world. For many monuments, the distinction should probably be not so much spiritual as opposed to practical, but one that stresses special places where activities outside the normal round of everyday activities took place. In many instances monuments were where rites of passage were performed, special places where people could act out rituals and ceremonies concerned with birth, puberty, marriage and death. These helped them deal with the stresses involved in transformation from one stage of life to the next. Some monuments were probably also used to celebrate natural transformations, such as the progression of the seasons, cyclical land fertility and astronomical events that go with the yearly round.

Many natural places, such as distinctive crags and springs, may have been seen as particularly sacred, and rituals and ceremonies probably took place there. Monuments are different from these in two ways. Firstly their building defines a special space that is overtly set apart from the everyday world, as much to protect people from what takes place there as to celebrate the specialness of that place. Architecture is also used to express ideas and beliefs. Thus, spectacular backdrops or containers for ceremonies can be created. These influence the way people think about and respond to the acts they are performing or witnessing. This influences not only acts in the spiritual realm, but in the way society is organised and manipulated socially and politically.

*Sacred Landscapes:
Monuments for the
Living and the
Dead*

A place for the ancestors: chambered cairns and long barrows

The earliest surviving earthworks in the region are monumental mounds of various designs. They were built in the Neolithic, between 4000 BC and 2000 BC. The best known are the chambered cairns, of which there are eight certain examples. These mounds contain chambers built of large stone slabs and drystone walling. Some are simple closed boxes, while others have low approach passages from the mound edge. The earliest mounds appear to be those that are relatively small and circular, with one or two chambers. Later, long mounds and massive near-circular mounds were built, both with several chambers. There are a further five certain long cairns with no known chambers. However, it is far from clear if wrecked or buried chambers would be found upon excavation (Figure 10; Colour Plate 1).

One large chambered cairn, at Minninglow on a high hilltop between Parwich and Elton, started life as a small mound with a chamber. It was later enveloped in a long cairn with at least four chambers entered from the sides. Later still it was enlarged again, to make it into a massive near-circular mound.

FIGURE 10
The Five Wells chambered cairn as it may have looked in prehistory. This reconstruction shows the site as it was first built, with two low entrances, at opposite sides, leading to low passages, which had to be crawled down to reach back to back chambers at the dark heart of the mound. The entrances to the passages may well have been blocked by stones which were cleared only when access to the bones of the ancestors was required for rites and ceremonies. Later in its life the site was altered, the features shown here being enveloped in a larger mound.

There are four or five such 'great barrows' in the region, each about 40m (131ft) across, which were probably the local equivalents of Later Neolithic mounds such as Silbury Hill near Avebury in Wiltshire and Duggleby Howe, on the Yorkshire Wolds. A related phenomenon in the Peak District, of which there are at least three examples, is the practice of superimposing Bronze Age round barrows at one end of long barrows. Another very unusual site, probably Later Neolithic, is Long Low near Wetton. This comprises an exceptional mound, 210m (689ft) long and 12–28m (40–92ft) wide. At the wider east end there is a possible horned forecourt and a collapsed and buried chamber (Figure 11).

Unfortunately virtually all the chambered sites in the Peak had their contents robbed or removed before being excavated by antiquarians. One possible exception is at Long Low, where although the chamber had either partly collapsed or had been disturbed, the floor was still covered with 13 or more overlapping skeletons, at least partly articulated, together with animal bones and three leaf-shaped arrowheads.

One characteristic of chambered sites throughout Britain is that while their external architecture is often similar, the chambers inside are more variable in design. This reflects the fact that while the outside could be copied by strangers, the interior was probably only ever seen by members of the community who built it. Chambers, where undisturbed, often contain bones of

FIGURE 11
Gib Hill, adjacent to Arbor Low. The original focus for ceremonial activity at Arbor Low, high on a ridgetop south of Monyash, was not at the large henge monument, but here at this mound. Careful examination of the mound's profile shows that it is a long barrow with a large circular mound superimposed at the south-western end to the right. The round barrow is Bronze Age in date, one of two built at this time overlying the main ceremonial monuments of the complex. This one contained a burial in a stone cist, placed at the surface of the earlier mound, which fell through the roof of Bateman's tunnel when he dug here in the middle of the nineteenth century. In the earlier mound underneath, probably built several centuries before the henge, early nineteenth-century excavations appear to have found cremated human bone in layers as well as scattered oxen bones.

Sacred Landscapes:
Monuments for the
Living and the
Dead

several individuals mixed together. The careful arrangement of bones at some sites, together with noticeable under-representation of specific parts of bodies, suggests the chambers were for bone storage, rather than the respectful burial of individual people in a modern sense. The chambers were probably designed as places where the bones of the ancestors were kept, sometimes to be periodically removed for ceremonies. That the chambers were often within impressive mounds suggests that, for the living, they were more than ossuaries, they were important symbols. They would be both focal points for the communities that built them and signals to outsiders that the group had traditional tenurial rights to the land; 'we can use these pastures, for look, here are our ancestors'.

Dealing with the ancestors was probably an act that people were fearful of. Burial of the bones in a special place safely separated them from everyday spheres. It may well be that rituals that took place within them was the realm of shamen. Crawling along a low passage into a dark chamber full of bones emphasised the otherworldliness of the place. The sensory deprivation of the darkness, and the heightened awareness induced by fear, were ideal for inducing states of trance and visions.

All the Peak District mounds noted above lie on the limestone plateau. It has traditionally been argued that this indicates that Neolithic settlement concentrated in this zone. However, it may be that monuments were built here for reasons to do with the character of the landscape, the use to which it was put and how people perceived it, rather than because the area was the settlement core. If the limestone plateau and parts of the gritstone uplands were used for seasonal grazing, then the need to establish tenure by reference to monuments holding the ancestors would be increased. The dichotomy of limestone plateau with monuments and gritstone upland without may be due to differences in topography and location. The limestone is at the centre, surrounded by valleys, and thus different groups coming in were likely to meet and thus be in competition for grazing rights. The gritstone upland in contrast is at the periphery and groups are more likely to only meet nearest neighbours.

Reinforcing communal identity: the Gardom's Edge enclosure

There is a large enclosure on Gardom's Edge above Baslow (see Figure 4). This has been recognised in recent years as being of Neolithic date, possibly built between 3500 BC and 3000 BC. It is a rare upland equivalent to the causewayed enclosures found in the lowlands of southern England. The Gardom's Edge enclosure has a massive bank built of boulders, in its collapsed and robbed state 5–9m (16–30ft) wide and 1.0–1.5m (3–5ft) high, with entrances spaced along it. It defines the eastern side of a large area at the crest of the ridge, the western side being the precipitous scarp overlooking the Derwent valley. The interior is largely boulder strewn and unsuitable for settlement, although there are a few places where buildings could have been erected.

A second enclosure, of similar character but defining a much smaller rocky prominence has been identified at Cratcliff Rocks on Harthill Moor, near the Nine Stone Close stone circle and Robin Hood's Stride (see below).

Interpreting causewayed enclosures and related sites is difficult, in that excavations have produced very different results from site to site. They were the most ambitious structures of their age in terms of size and complexity, and thus almost certainly tribal meeting places that were multi-purpose in character. While some developed defensive characteristics, this was probably not their main purpose. Equally, they were not normal settlements, but often had a range of special activities associated with them. These included feasting, exchange of exotic raw materials, and the exposure of the newly dead prior to the burial of their bones. The building of banks was perhaps more to define a special area excluded from the everyday world, than to keep outsiders at bay. In part they may have been built to contain activities that were found threatening to the everyday fabric of society and thus they are often placed at the edges of settled areas rather than at their heart.

Tribal and family rites: henges and stone circles

There is a strong contrast between the two massive henge monuments found on the limestone plateau and the large number of small stone circles on the eastern gritstone upland.

The henges, Arbor Low near Monyash and the Bull Ring at Dove Holes, were probably built in the Later Neolithic, between 3000 BC and 2000 BC. They are very similar monuments to each other, both in size and design, though the Bull Ring had its stone settings removed in the eighteenth century. Both these circular areas are defined by banks with internal quarry ditches. They are large enough to hold many people and between them, the two henges were probably used by many, if not all the region's communities (Colour Plates 2 and 3).

The small stone circles and related structures, of which there are 26 certain examples in the Peak District, were probably built in the few hundred years either side of 2000 BC. Nearly all comprise a ring of small upright stones set on the inner edge of a bank, a monument form most common here but also found throughout northern England and Wales. Nine Stone Close on Harthill Moor, west of Birchover, stands out as different to the rest, with its small diameter but tall stones. Several other circles had one taller stone in the ring. A few Peak District circles have no bank, while others today have only a bank but no standing stones. At several excavated examples the internal areas have been found to contain buried human cremations, sometimes in urns (Figure 12; Colour Plate 4).

The large henges are obviously communal monuments. Because the small stone circles sometimes contain burials, some have suggested they are nothing more than fancy burial monuments. This is much like saying parish churches are only tombs because they contain graves. The archaeological evidence is biased, for of all the ceremonies concerned with rites of passage at birth,

FIGURE 12

The Barbrook II stone circle. This small stone circle is one of two that lie within a large cairnfield on Ramsley Moor, which is that part of the Big Moor complex lying to the east of Bar Brook. It was extensively excavated in the 1960s and restored in 1989. The circle is now probably much as it was around 2000 BC. The irregular ring of standing stones is set in a drystone wall retaining the inner edge of a rubble bank, with an entrance to the north-east. Only one standing stone is significantly higher than the bank. This lies a little south of west and has no obvious astronomical explanation. Although a variety of rituals and ceremonies probably took place at the circle, it is those connected with death that not surprisingly have left traces in the ground. Four human cremations were deposited in the south-western half of the interior, two in simple pits, one in a pit under a small cairn, and one in a small stone burial box known as a cist.

puberty, marriage and death, it is only the last which normally leaves deposits in the ground. Equally, seasonal celebrations could have taken place for centuries without leaving any trace.

Stone circles have been controversial monuments for many years because of theories concerning geometric layout and astronomical alignment connected with them. While strong arguments can be put forward to support the idea that geometric layout is an ethnocentric suggestion and that the rings were normally laid out by eye to appear circular, there is good evidence to support a link with astronomy at some stone circles. The most convincing evidence is alignments that looked impressive at certain times of year, such as solstices, where the sun or moon rose or set behind large erected stones or prominent natural features (Figure 13).

Many of the structures built in Britain between 3000 BC and 1500 BC, ranging from houses to stone circles and tombs, reflect an obsession with circular architecture. Circular structures perhaps reflect community as opposed to hierarchy in that they hold people equally, whereas square or rectangular buildings are sometimes more suitable for focusing on such things as altars or thrones

FIGURE 13

The Nine Stone Close stone circle with Robin Hood's Stride in the background. It is probably not coincidence that this small stone circle was sited near the impressive natural outcrop of Robin Hood's Stride, on Harthill Moor, itself probably regarded as a sacred place in prehistory. The crag forms an impressive backdrop to ceremonies that would have taken place at the ring. Around midsummer the full moon is low in the sky and would have passed between the two natural pillars. The circle today has four tall stones but originally there were eight or nine, the missing ones removed in the last two hundred and fifty years.

at one end, with the entrance at the other. The societies that built stone circles used them to symbolise their communal identity rather than the power of individual leaders. Circular structures may also symbolise celestial bodies such as sun or moon.

Both henges and small stone circles have one thing in common: unlike chambered tombs and barrows, they are essentially open sites designed to hold the living. In the case of the henges this may have been whole tribes, whereas the small circles may have been family or kin group monuments. On the eastern moorlands the circles and ringcairns are always found in direct association with the fields and cairnfields discussed in Chapter 2. Each local community had both its own circle and barrow, catering for the living and the dead.

Rites for the dead: barrows and cremation cemeteries

Over 500 barrows have been identified across the region. These were probably mostly built in the period 2500 BC–1500 BC, spanning the Later Neolithic and Earlier Bronze Age. Virtually all are circular mounds of earth and stone, normally no more than 30m (98ft) across. Now mostly grass-covered mounds, originally they may have stood out, for example, as gleaming white mounds of limestone or as kerb-retained heaps of gritstone boulders. At a few large barrows there are signs of silted quarry ditches surrounding mounds. One very unusual site, at Hob Hurst's House on Harland Edge above Beeley, is square with a bank and ditch surrounding a mound with a large central stone cist. Smaller mounds were most likely built from surface-gathered stones and turves, perhaps cut when established pastures were periodically converted to arable.

Many of the region's barrows were excavated in the 1840s and 1850s by Thomas Bateman and Samuel Carrington. They found many kerbs, cists and rock-cut graves beneath barrows. Modern excavations have shown that mounds were often enlarged over time. It is also clear that, before mounds were built, the sites functioned as open ritual areas, often defined by kerbs or hurdlework fences. Mounds were usually not built until after several burials had been deposited. It is not clear if this time lag was only a matter of months, or whether the sites remained open for many years. It may even be that the building of the mound effectively closed the site down, or more probably moved it into a new phase with different rituals (Figure 14).

Bateman and Carrington mostly dug on the limestone plateau, where bones often survive in relatively alkaline soils. Thus a large amount of information was recovered on how people were buried. Burial of both unburnt bodies and cremated bones was practised. Bodies were often placed on their sides in a flexed or contracted foetal position. Not all the scattered human bones commonly found in barrows are from disturbed burials. At an excavated barrow on Wigber Low near Kniveton, it has been demonstrated that the mound was used as an exposure platform, where bodies were left to rot on the surface. The bones, except for a few that fell amongst the stones of the cairn, were later

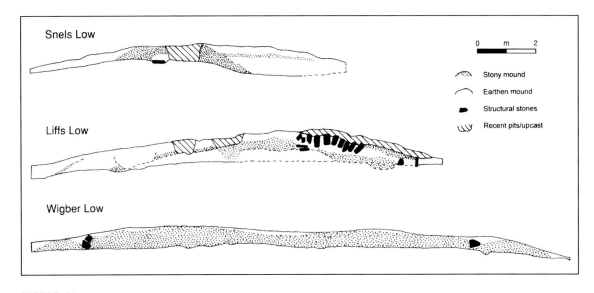

FIGURE 14

Sections through multi-phased barrows at Liffs Low, Snels Low and Wigber Low. Many barrows in the Peak District were probably enlarged at least once, although the evidence for this is usually only found by modern excavation techniques. Three such excavations illustrate the range of variety. Snels Low, at Peak Forest, started life as a cairn over a crouched inhumation that was subsequently enlarged in earth. Liffs Low, near Biggin, began as a Later Neolithic earthen barrow over a cist, with a crouched inhumation accompanied by a particularly fine suite of artefacts (Colour Plate 5). It was later enlarged to the south in earth, while to north there was a layered enlargement over a grave pit. This had a unique setting of concentric slabs on the crest and a covering of small angular stones on the side terminating at a kerb. Wigber Low, near Kniveton, started life as a kerbed exposure platform, later enlarged, with prehistoric and then Anglian burials added.

removed from site. The position of intact burials within barrows varied, ranging from pits or rock-cut graves under mounds, through placement on the buried ground surface, to positions high in the mound. Cists that gave added protection or importance were used in all three positions. It used to be thought that round barrows contained one 'primary' burial and that all others were 'secondary' and therefore less important. Bateman's belief in this theory significantly biased the evidence, for he would normally dig at the centre of a mound until he found a grave with grave goods which he thought signified the burial of a 'chieftain' and then he stopped digging. More-complete excavation of Peak District barrows has revealed a very different picture. Barrows, unless very small, usually contain several primary burials, with totals often in the range five to twenty. These are similar numbers to those for the region's chambered cairns, but with one important difference. While the bones in the earlier mounds are mixed, or at least placed together in a chamber, there is greater emphasis on burial of individual bodies in the later mounds (Figure 15).

Burials are often accompanied by grave goods, a wide variety of which have been recovered. However, in contrast with areas like Wessex, where some burials are found accompanied by gold or gold-decorated ornaments and other

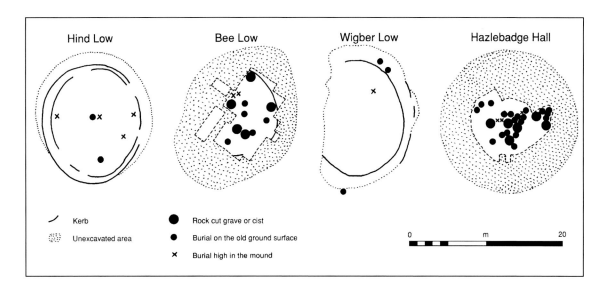

Barrows with multiple burial deposits at Hind Low, Bee Low, Wigber Low and Hazlebadge Hall. The majority of extensively-excavated round barrows in the Peak District contain several burials, often with more than one with grave goods of equal complexity. Hind Low barrow, south-east of Buxton, had several inhumations placed on the old ground surface, mostly at a point south of its centre. Some of the bodies had been there some time and were far from complete when the primary kerbed mound was built. Further bone deposits were made when the mound was built, and again when it was refurbished and an outer kerb added. Bee Low barrow, near Youlgrave, and Hazlebadge Hall barrow, near Bradwell, had a variety of burials, some in cists or rock-cut graves, some accompanied with grave goods such as beakers and food vessels, bronze knives and awls. The main mound at Wigber Low, near Kniveton, covered no primary burials, but was used as an exposure platform for at least 21 individuals, as indicated by fragments of bone that were recovered from between the stones of the mound. Prehistoric burials were later incorporated around the site edge when the mound was enlarged. Anglian graves were also added, which are not shown.

'fancy' objects, very few 'rich' graves are found in the Peak District. No objects of gold are known. Normally, where grave-goods are present at all, they are few and relatively simple, such as bone pins, stone tools, crudely decorated pots, beads or buttons and natural objects such as quartz pebbles or lumps of ochre. Some urns held cremations, while other pots contained ritual offerings of food or drink. Occasionally, finely made objects accompanied burials, such as bronze daggers and axes, stone battle-axes and jet necklaces. Only two burials in the whole region had rich suites of artefacts. At Liffs Low near Biggin, a Neolithic cist grave contained an adult male skeleton accompanied by an antler macehead, a small pottery flask, two boar's tusk knives, pieces of red ochre, two edge-polished flint axes, two lozenge-shaped flint arrowheads, a flint saw, three flint knives and assorted other flints. At Green Low, 2km (1.2 miles) to the south, there was a Bronze Age rock-cut grave with an adult male skeleton, accompanied by the bones of an infant, a beaker, a flint dagger, five barbed and tanged arrowheads, a plano-convex knife and other flints, three bone spatulae, a bone pin and a piece of iron pyrites (Colour Plate 5).

Far fewer grave goods are found with cremations than with inhumations. It used to be thought that cremations represented the burials of less important individuals. This may well be untrue. What was buried with the bones does not necessarily reflect what accompanied the body on the funeral pyre, many objects could have been then destroyed, removed or simply not buried with the bones. More fundamentally, most grave goods in any case are unlikely to be fixed indicators of status. Few of the objects have any great intrinsic worth. Value put on objects changes with distance from source and is downgraded through time with familiarity. Objects placed with graves may not have been displays of wealth, but objects that represented the role of the individual in life and which passed on the correct messages from the living to the spirit world. They also show how the living thought of the dead and reflect the re-negotiation of the social roles of the living after the death of one of their community.

Far more round barrows were built than the earlier chambered cairns. This may be explained by the different social dimension in which each type of monument operated. Chambered cairns appear to have been used by tribal groups as a whole, while barrows were more local in focus, probably built by individual family communities, of which there were many in the region. The emphasis changed from ancestors buried together to lineage and ancestry, with family representatives buried individually.

Even though round barrows contain several burials, and some barrows have been lost, it is very likely that in the thousand years or so over which they were built and used, far fewer than one individual per generation in any given local community was given a barrow burial. Thus, those buried in barrows were not members of elite groups all of whom had automatic right to barrow burial. Burials include people of all ages and both sexes. As artefacts do not reflect status, burials could be of people regarded as having shamanistic powers, or more broadly, people chosen to represent the local group as a whole. If, as seems probable, barrows continued to demonstrate claims on land, they may include founder members of families. Subsequent burial may have been restricted to times of crisis, when the need for re-affirmation was felt. A range of different crises can be envisaged, from bad crop yields to encroachment of powerful new neighbours or changes in family allegiance.

FIGURE 16 (*opposite*)
The cairnfields on Stanton Moor, Raven Tor and Gibbet Moor. Three cairnfields in the Peak District show atypical signs of being overtly funerary in function. They have a high proportion of small mounds with formal architectural characteristics such as kerbs, and some are rectangular in shape. Others are abutted to each other to form complex monuments. The small cairnfields at Raven Tor and Gibbet Moor, above Beeley, are at exposed hilltop locations not ideal for agricultural exploitation. The northern part of Stanton Moor, above Stanton, has agricultural clearance features overlain by a later field system of uncertain date, whereas on the higher parts of the moor to the south, the cairns appear to be funerary in character. Selected sites at Stanton Moor and Raven Tor have been excavated and cremations found, some with urns and other funerary goods. Many of the excavations on Stanton Moor were carried out by the Heathcote family. Of the published sites, 19 small cairns had burials, while only one didn't. Of the approximately 20 unpublished cairn excavations, only four produced recognisable grave goods that survive in the Heathcote collection in Sheveld City Museum.

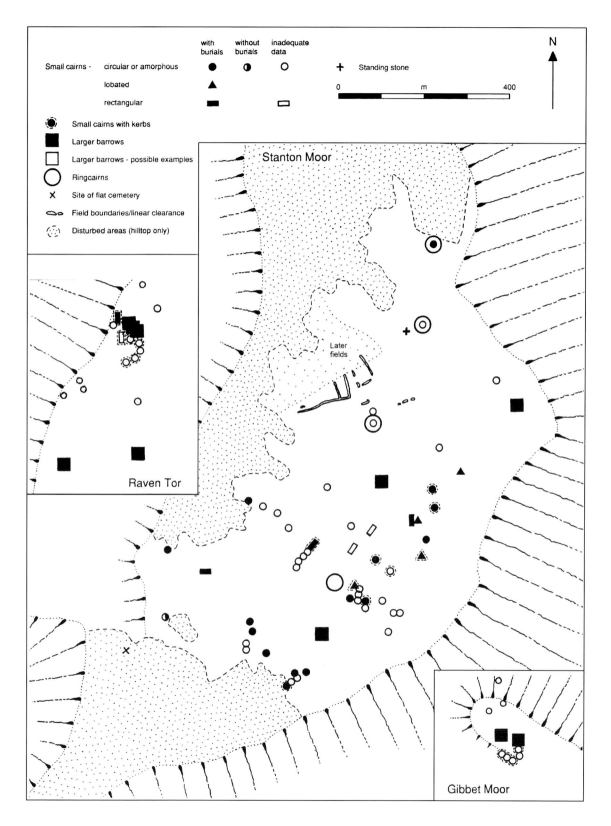

Small cairns - circular or amorphous
lobated
rectangular

with burials
without burials
inadequate data

Standing stone

Small cairns with kerbs
Larger barrows
Larger barrows - possible examples
Ringcairns
Site of flat cemetery
Field boundaries/linear clearance
Disturbed areas (hilltop only)

0   m   400

N

Stanton Moor

Later fields

Raven Tor

Gibbet Moor

37

We rarely get glimpses of what happened after death to those not buried in barrows. Sites on the eastern gritstone moors are an exception to this. It was noted in Chapter 2 that a proportion of the small cairns in agricultural cairnfields contain ritual deposits and human burials. In three exceptional cases there are cairnfields that may be primarily funerary. Two, on Gibbet Moor and Raven Tor, both above Beeley, have only a few cairns. The third on Stanton Moor, above Stanton, is much larger and is better known because of the excavations by the Heathcotes. A further type of burial site was demonstrated when, in the 1920s, a cemetery of cremations in urns with no cairn above was discovered accidentally by quarrymen near the south-western edge of Stanton Moor. An equally accidental discovery was made on Eaglestone Flat, above Baslow, in the 1980s, when a drain cut through a complex cemetery. Burials were found both with and without associated stone features. Open cemeteries may be relatively common but rarely found because they are undetectable at the surface. Other ways of disposing of the dead, such as exposure, leave even slighter archaeological evidence (Figures 9 and 16, Colour Plate 6).

A place to leave your mark: prehistoric rock art in the Peak

The Peak District does not have large quantities of the enigmatic prehistoric cup and ring art, as found further north on Rombalds Moor near Ilkley, in Northumberland and Scotland. However, there are several good examples, as at a large slab on Gardom's Edge and two recently unburied examples at Ashover School. Other portable examples have been found during excavations at barrows and stone circles.

Monuments in the landscape: their place in later prehistoric society

Because much of the prehistoric landscape on the eastern gritstone moors can be reconstructed, this allows exceptional insights into how people there organised themselves. Each of the small communities had their own fields together with stone circles and barrows within or near the edge of the fields. The only monuments also found at a distance from the settlements are barrows. These tend to be close to topographical boundaries, placed to either side of watersheds rather than on them and thus sited specifically to overlook the grazing areas of the communities which built them. Occasionally, glimpses are gained of the distinctiveness of local communities. For example, on Gibbet Moor above Chatsworth the local farmers chose to build several small standing-stone settings, each with between two and four stones, rather than the larger stone circles of their neighbours (Figure 17).

If, as seems to be the case, every local community on the eastern gritstone upland had its own barrow, then this has implications for ideas about the status of the individuals buried in such monuments, both here and on the limestone plateau. There is no difference in the nature or quality of grave goods between the two zones. Indeed, barrows are even more common on the

Sacred Landscapes:
Monuments for the
Living and the
Dead

limestone plateau, where they occur in small numbers throughout. It used to be thought that barrows contained the burials of chiefs or other important tribal leaders. The evidence from the Peak District suggests it is more likely that the people buried here are representatives of ordinary farming families.

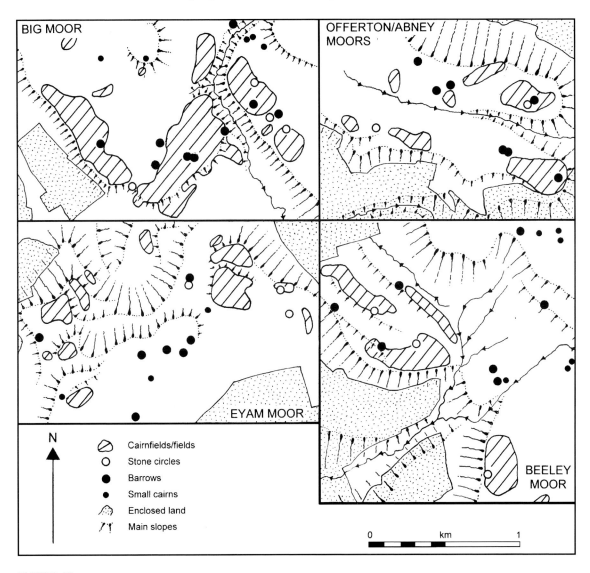

FIGURE 17

Examples of the relationship between monuments and settlement on the gritstone moors. All stone circles and most barrows are found in close proximity to the later prehistoric fields of the gritstone upland, except where later agriculture has removed the remains of prehistoric clearance, leaving only the larger monuments. The siting of monuments is non-random. They are commonly found near the edges of the agricultural areas, as at Big Moor, north-east of Baslow, and Eyam Moor, with a tendency also to be at the ends of elongated systems, as at Offerton/Abney Moors and Beeley Moor. When within fields, as on Big Moor, barrows are located centrally. On Eyam Moor and Beeley Moor barrows also exist in small cemeteries on land set apart from the fields. On Harland Edge, above the prehistoric fields of Beeley Moor, there are two large barrows at a distance close to the watershed, sited to overlook the land of the living.

Although tribal leaders are invisible in the grave goods found within barrows, this does not mean they did not exist. That the henges at Arbor Low and the Bull Ring were built at all indicates large-scale co-operation at a tribal level at the time that unchambered round barrows were first being built. Similarly the other large Later Neolithic monuments, the 'great barrows' and Long Low, required such communal effort.

Paradoxically, the strongest remaining symbol of the presence of an elite is the round barrow built on the bank of the Arbor Low henge. It lies on the upslope side of the monument, opposite the main entrance, and dominates the interior of the site. It represents a rare example of a monument being used overtly to manipulate society. It was built at a time of social transformation, at the start of the rise of the power of the individual, a process which led eventually to the establishment of hereditary elites with significant power over other members of society. While the presence of the barrow shows one family dominated communal gatherings here, it is significant that the site continued to be used. Power was legitimised by claiming ownership of a site that symbolised the traditional communal ways.

After well over a thousand years of intensive monument building, in the centuries after 1500 BC they ceased to be built. This probably occurred after the new social order was firmly established, and thus overt and labour intensive monumental symbols were no longer necessary. With the increasingly locally-focussed and perhaps sedentary nature of farming which developed from around 2000 BC onwards, the 'ownership' of land became fixed and did not need monuments as reminders of traditional rights. With the establishment of a hierarchical society with a ruling elite, and with the increasingly subservient position of most families, monuments that stood for family and local community became increasingly anachronistic.

CHAPTER FOUR

After a Worsening in the Weather: Later Prehistory and the Coming of the Romans

Protecting declining resources: hillforts overlooking settled valleys

The last thousand years BC, all but the earliest centuries of which are known as the Iron Age, saw changes in the settlement of the region. The climate was deteriorating, becoming cooler and wetter. Many of the more exposed farms and fields on the gritstone eastern moors were eventually abandoned. Analysis of pollen in peat cores in this area show there was a decrease in tree pollen. In part, this probably reflects significant clearance of the lowland woodlands of the Derwent valley and of the Pennine foothills to the east. However, some of the tree pollen probably derived from the local upland environment. The disappearance of trees is unlikely to be the product of clearance if the farms of the area were being deserted. It may be that the abandonment of the farms itself was the catalyst for the changes in vegetation, leading to the growing out of hedges and decline of woodlands due to lack of management and changes in grazing patterns. Unrestricted but low levels of upland grazing, as practised to the present day, keep woodland from regenerating on the eastern moors.

It is unclear to what extent the climatic decline led to a fall in the region's population. It may be that the traditional settlement areas on the limestone plateau shelves were better suited to withstand the changes. People displaced from the gritstones may have moved to places like the sheltered Derwent Valley, clearing these further rather than leaving the region. The main problem with assessing these possibilities is that the Iron Age population probably inhabited those areas which continued to be cultivated through to the present day. Buried archaeological evidence is invisible due to paucity of diagnostic artefacts and a present lack of cereal cultivation and therefore extensive evidence from cropmark photographs.

The one exception to this lack of data is the hillforts. That monuments display overtly defensive characteristics is an illustration of the stress on the population at this time. By the time of the Roman invasions, tribal society in Britain had developed a number of kingdoms and loose confederations of tribes, each ruled by hereditary elites who controlled resources. Cattle appear

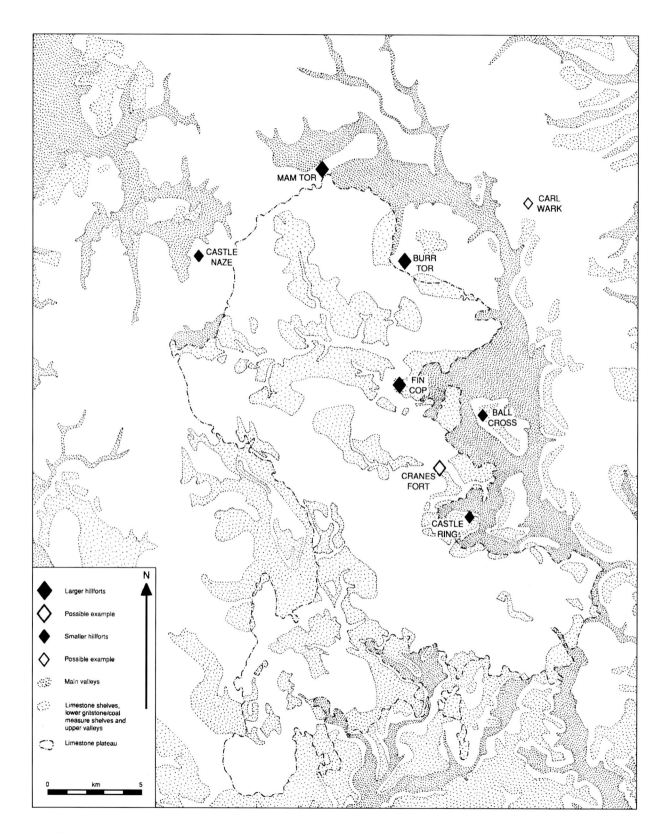

CARL
WARK

MAM TOR

CASTLE
NAZE

BURR
TOR

FIN
COP

BALL
CROSS

CRANES
FORT

CASTLE
RING

N

◆ Larger hillforts

◇ Possible example

◆ Smaller hillforts

◇ Possible example

Main valleys

Limestone shelves,
lower gritstone/coal
measure shelves and
upper valleys

Limestone plateau

0   km   5

*After a Worsening
in the Weather:
Later Prehistory and
the Coming of the
Romans*

to have been of particular importance as a form of mobile wealth. Hillforts were frequently larger and more heavily defensive than practicality demanded. They were demonstrations of power and prestige which can be seen as the nuclear deterrents of the Iron Age. The scale and character of any actual warfare remains a matter for debate. For much of the time there was probably little physical conflict, rather, many hillforts no doubt acted as focal centres for local tribes and their leaders, the ramparts highly visible expressions of their status and strength.

Only eight hillforts at most exist in the Peak District, usually defined by a single rampart comprising a large bank with external ditch. Exceptions are a double rampart at Castle Naze, above Chapel en le Frith, and a vertically-faced rampart without ditch at the undated site of Carl Wark, above Hathersage. Some of the smaller sites may be little more than enclosed settlements (Figure 18).

The large hillforts of the region, at Mam Tor, near Castleton; Burr Tor, above Great Hucklow; Fin Cop, above Ashford; and possibly the uncertainly interpreted Cranes Fort, near Youlgreave, each lie above what are likely to have been focal settlement areas in later prehistory. Three are centred on relatively sheltered basins around the main rivers, at the interface with complementary resource areas on the limestone plateau and gritstone uplands. The fourth, at Burr Tor, high on one corner of an upland gritstone moor, overlooks a relatively sheltered area of the limestone plateau between Eyam and Hazlebadge. This fort, while large in area, was only slightly defended and it may be that it was abandoned earlier than the others, as continuing climatic deterioration led to the lessening importance of its territory. Mam Tor, the only one of the four to have been excavated, creates a parallel in that it started life as a slightly defended site, but was later rebuilt with stronger ramparts. All but Cranes Fort are on visually prominent hilltops when viewed from the settlement areas below, emphasising their impressiveness (Figures 19, 20, 21).

The Mam Tor hillfort is exceptional in that its interior mostly consists of sloping rather than flat land. These slopes have over one hundred scoops cut into them. Small-scale excavations have demonstrated some at least to be terraced platforms that supported circular houses. Two charcoal samples gave Bronze Age radiocarbon dates falling somewhere in the period 1700 BC to 1000 BC. However, these samples amalgamated scattered charcoal, analysed at a time when procedures for this method of dating were in their infancy; this would not be done today and the dates should be treated with great caution. Taken at face value, these dates are particularly early for a hillfort. Thus, it may be settlement started before the ramparts were built. Alternatively, some of the charcoal may be from activity on the hilltop that predated settlement, thus

FIGURE 18 (*opposite*)
Map showing the hillforts of the Peak District. This map illustrates a correlation between hillforts, particularly the larger ones, and the main areas in which Iron Age settlement is likely to have taken place. The majority lie close to the interface between the limestone plateau land beyond, thus having access to contrasting resources areas. Further major settlement areas to the south have no known associated hillforts.

FIGURE 19

The Mam Tor hillfort. This fine site at the head of the Hope valley dominates the surrounding landscape. The landslip scars were probably already present when it was built, but subsequent erosion has slightly truncated the defensive earthworks. These consist of a single rampart, outer ditch, and a counterscarp bank probably formed from periodic cleaning of the ditch. These may well have been intended as a display of strength and prestige rather than a reflection of a real need to defend the occupants. Excavation has shown that the earliest 'defences' were probably a timber palisade with ditch, later replaced with a rampart with vertical stone-faced side, which later still was strengthened near the entrances. Two inturned entrances allow access to the interior which is covered by many small platforms terraced into the slopes. Excavations have found circular buildings here. There were also two hilltop barrows within the fort which may well have been built before the earliest settlement.

FIGURE 20

The Fin Cop hillfort as it may have looked in later prehistory. This large hillfort on the high crest of Fin Cop, above Ashford, is heavily 'defended' on one half, while at the other this was not necessary because of the deep gorge to the River Wye below. The impressive 'defences' face the lower Wye basin where the majority of people who built the fort probably lived and farmed. The site has never been excavated, hence the degree to which the interior was occupied is not known. A recently identified possible outwork may have been built to corral stock in times of trouble.

skewing the dates. The Mam Tor ramparts remain undated. Excavations at both Mam Tor and at Ball Cross, above Bakewell, have produced coarse pottery thought to date from the centuries around 1000 BC, while the style of the Mam Tor ramparts suggests a date several centuries later.

Not all hillforts in Britain were extensively occupied. Others were apparently used only in times of stress, or as places for storing surplus resources. Some sites may have had only temporary, perhaps seasonal occupancy. In contrast, other hillforts were occupied for many centuries. The lack of complex earthworks of later Iron Age type at the Peak District hillforts may suggest they had been abandoned centuries before the Romans arrived.

FIGURE 21
The massive defensive wall at Carl Wark. The boulder-strewn crag east of Hathersage on which this small 'fort' is built is naturally defensible on all sides but one. One of the steeper slopes has been enhanced along parts of its crest by the addition of a line of boulders. The one side that does not fall away steeply is blocked by a high rampart, faced on the outside by a drystone wall built of massive blocks and slabs. The interior is strewn with rock outcrops and boulders, leaving little room for buildings. The date of this site has always been a mystery, it being unlike any other structure in northern England. The only settlements in the immediate vicinity, on lower land to the south and west, are of third- to first-millennium BC type. The possibility that Carl Wark may be a particularly early site, perhaps of Neolithic or Bronze Age date, should not be ignored.

FIGURE 22 (*opposite*)
Map showing the location of Roman military works and civil centres, and native Romano-British settlements, in the Peak District. The known native settlements survive around the fringes of the traditional settlement zones. Superimposed are forts and military roads. Evidence for the lead industry, in the form of lead pigs, concentrates to the south-east and the administrative centre for this industry, the lost Lutodarum, may have been in this vicinity.

Enforcing a new order: the Roman occupation

The Roman army probably first entered the Peak District shortly before, or at the advent of, Agricola's push north into Brigantian territory in the late 70s AD. The forts of Navio and Ardotalia, which survive at Brough in the Hope valley and Melandra near Glossop, may have been built to support this expansion. Alternatively, it may be that permanent Roman occupation of the Peak

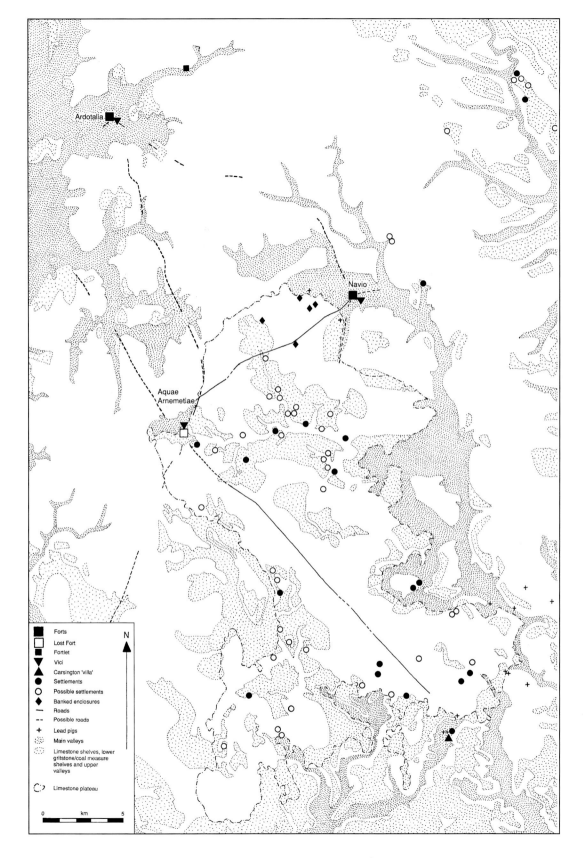

Ardotalia ■▼

Navio ■▼

Aquae
Arnemetiae ▼□

N
▲

	Forts
■	Forts
□	Lost Fort
■	Fortlet
▼	Vici
▲	Carsington 'villa'
●	Settlements
○	Possible settlements
◆	Banked enclosures
—	Roads
---	Possible roads
+	Lead pigs
	Main valleys
	Limestone shelves, lower gritstone/coal measure shelves and upper valleys
⌒	Limestone plateau

0   km   5

47

District did not take place until the 80s AD. The occupation was valuable to the Romans for a number of reasons, including securing the lead that the Peak District was known to contain; controlling the east-west route across the Peak through the Hope valley; and, initially, to secure the area to the rear of the advancing Roman armies as they moved further north.

Both Navio and Ardotalia had thriving civil settlements, which grew up outside their gates to provide services and amenities for the garrisons. The Peak District's forts were part of a network built across the country, linked by military roads. A possible third fort at Buxton has been assumed on the basis of the military road network but no evidence for its existence has so far been found. The military roads often comprised raised hard-core causeways, with ditches to either side. They were built in short straight stretches, with frequent changes of angle necessary to negotiate the difficult local topography (Figure 22).

In the first half of the second century the forts in the Peak District were abandoned. With the building of Hadrian's Wall, and the Antonine pushes into Scotland, all available troops were needed further north. However, Navio was rebuilt in AD 154–8, after a possible Brigantian revolt, and continued to be occupied until the mid-fourth century. There was a gradual withdrawal of the Roman military and administration from Britain in the early fifth century.

The fort at Brough lies at the heart of the Hope valley and may well have been purposefully sited at the centre of one of the focal areas of native population in the region. It was also sited strategically to control access east-west along the Hope valley as well as southwards through Bradwell Dale into the heart of the lead orefield. Some evidence suggests that its vicus (civilian settlement) continued to be occupied during the time the fort was abandoned in the first half of the second century. There was a second important urban site at the spa centre of Aquae Arnemetiae, focused on the mineral springs at Buxton. Votive deposits at the springs show they were venerated by the first century AD and continued in use into the fourth century.

There is little evidence for the local elite of the Roman period, the possible exception being at an excavated building at Carsington. This stone dwelling, perhaps best described as a small villa, had two wings, one a bath suite with hypocaust heating. The building was erected in the fourth century, although there was earlier occupation on site from the second century onwards. Anglo-Saxon pottery of fifth- to sixth-century date has been found in the ditch that surrounds the complex.

Few structures of the Roman occupation survive above ground. At Brough and Melandra the outlines of the fortifications can be traced as earthworks. Aquae Arnemetiae lies under modern Buxton. Short stretches of modern roads between Buxton and Brough, and Buxton and Ashbourne, follow the course of Roman roads. Elsewhere on these same routes slight earthworks can be seen running through fields. The so-called Roman road at Long Causeway above Stanage Edge, between Bamford and Sheffield, is eighteenth century in date (Colour Plate 7).

*After a Worsening
in the Weather:
Later Prehistory and
the Coming of the
Romans*

The discovery of hidden wealth: early mining

The recent discovery of hammerstones and a radiocarbon-dated antler tool demonstrate that copper was mined in the Earlier Bronze Age at Ecton Hill near Warslow. Similarly, lead may well have been mined in small quantities at various sites on the limestone plateau, as indicated by the discovery of lead artefacts at Mam Tor and Gardom's Edge which date to the Later Bronze Age or Early Iron Age. However, with the coming of the Romans to Britain the lead ores took on new importance because of the small percentage of silver they often contained. This was used for coinage and prestige objects, and thus the ores were an important source of wealth. The lead itself was also used for such things as pewter artefacts, as well as cisterns and water pipes for civic and military buildings. Whether the local lead ores contained silver is a matter of debate. The ores from post-medieval mines contained very little, but this may reflect selective mining of silver-rich deposits at an earlier date. The main evidence for Roman mining in the Peak District comes from the accidental discovery of cast ingots or pigs both here and elsewhere in Britain. Often these have inscriptions that identify them as from the region and also indicate that any silver had already been removed. The mines themselves are generally elusive, because later miners have cut through these earlier shallow workings to get to remaining ore below, dumping their spoil over earlier heaps. Previous claims for Roman galleries at various show caves are unfounded. The workings in question are at best undatable, being anything from Roman to seventeenth century in date. It has been suggested that a stretch of second-century AD field wall at Roystone Grange near Ballidon overlay a working in a small lead vein. However, re-assessment of the wall has cast doubt on its date; it may be medieval.

Lutodarum, the documented probable administrative centre for the lead mining industry, is lost, but a location on or near the southern part of the limestone plateau with good access to the south, seems likely. An excavated site at Carsington has been suggested. While this remains an interesting possibility, particularly in the light of the excavated 'villa' nearby, it is unproven and other locations should be considered in the Wirksworth or Matlock areas. Another possibility is that Lutodarum denotes the name of a company contracted to carry out the mining rather than a specific place.

Away from the fort: the native farmed landscape

The native farmsteads of the Romano-British period in the Peak District were very different from the military and administrative settlements described above. They retained the general character of the farms of Iron Age Britain but contain evidence of the benefits of the Roman occupation enjoyed by the native population despite the taxes that would have been levied on the local people. This evidence includes such items as better quality ceramics and jewellery, reflecting the buoyant economy in the first and second centuries AD, created by the increased market opportunities that became available locally and further afield. Lead and perhaps silver from the Peak was exported afar. A further important source of income was the supplying of food to the Roman garrisons. Recession in the Roman empire in later years is equally reflected in poorer quality ceramics and a lack of such indicators of material wealth as jewellery and containers for wine.

The evidence for Iron Age origins for individual Romano-British settlements in the Peak District has as yet proved mostly elusive, due to the lack of extensive excavations, which makes it difficult to assess the impact of occupation on any native population. It is not known whether the occupation was resisted, welcomed or ignored. What is known is that, typically, the Peak District sites of Romano-British date comprise nucleated hamlets or farmsteads with several circular or rectangular buildings, together with associated yards, garden plots and lanes. Surrounding these are fields defined today by banks, sometimes with large stones set along both edges. The fields are often small and vary in shape from nearly square to sets of parallel narrow strips. The best known example of such a settlement is that at Roystone Grange, near Ballidon, which has been extensively studied by Sheffield University. However,

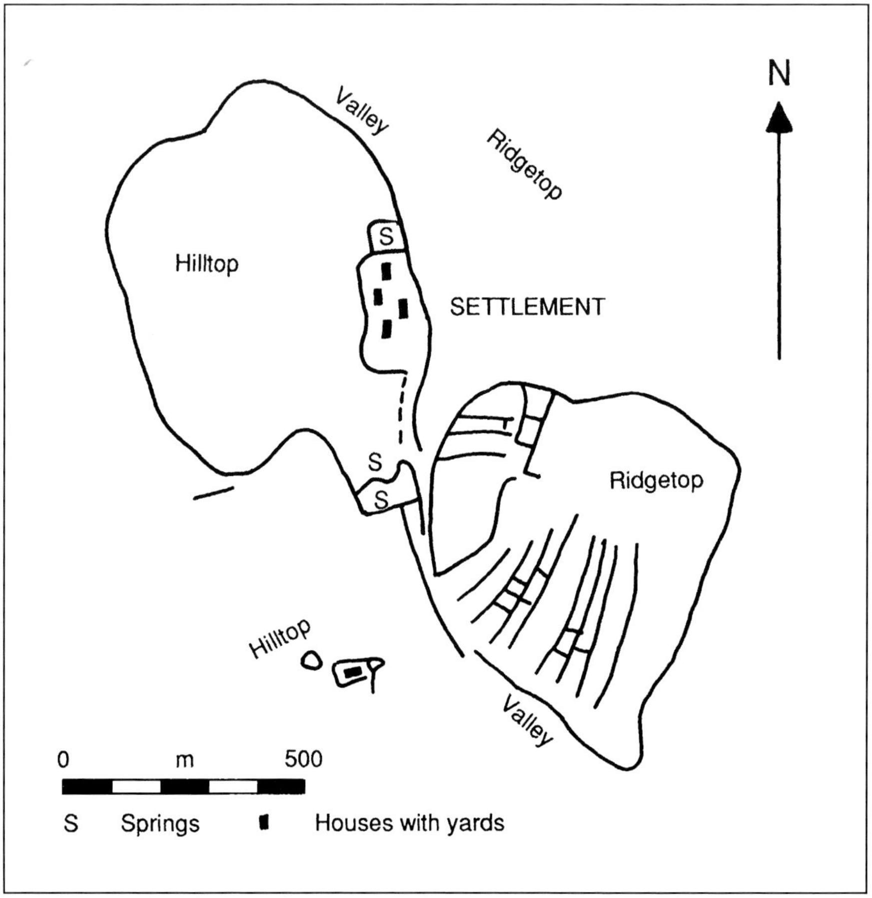

FIGURE 23
The native Romano-British farm at Roystone Grange near Ballidon. Excavations by Sheffield University have allowed reconstruction of the nature of settlement in this isolated dry valley from prehistory to the present day. In Roman times, from the second to fourth centuries AD, there was a small settlement near the valley bottom, with buildings terraced into the slope. This was possibly associated with two large enclosures taking in valley-side and higher land, although an alternate date in the medieval period should also be considered. One of these enclosures contains a series of narrow fields on the steep hillside, suggesting arable cultivation, while the other may have been used for winter grazing. Elsewhere the surrounding land appears to have mostly been open grazing, although this area also contained an isolated building in a small enclosure high above the valley.

FIGURE 24
The Romano-British settlement on Chee Tor near Blackwell. This well-preserved site has been saved from later agricultural destruction because of its location on a rocky spur surrounded by the deep Wye gorge on three sides. The settlement is visible as a series of lynchets and low stony banks. These define several rectangular yards and probable house sites, with short lanes between, and adjacent small fields or garden plots. Limited excavations have produced artefacts of third- and fourth-century AD date, and a burial under a small cairn in the corner of one of the enclosures.

well-preserved earthworks also occur at several other sites, including those on Chee Tor near Blackwell, at North Lees near Hathersage, and at Bank Top near Hartington (Figures 23, 24, 25).

Earthworks defining the buildings of Romano-British farmsteads and the fields that surround them have survived at around 50 locations in the region. They mostly occur on the limestone plateau, on the fringes of traditional settlement zones well established since at least the climatic decline of later prehistory. They survive in locations where later farming activity has not obliterated the surface evidence. In contrast, the majority of Romano-British farms that probably once existed on the most favourable parts of the limestone shelves and in the shale valleys have now been lost. Their sites could be found

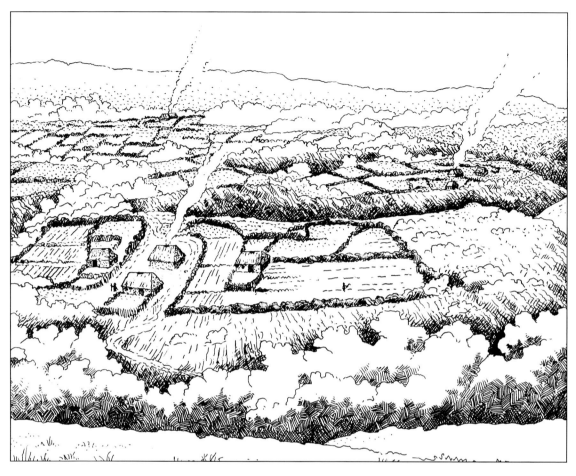

FIGURE 25

A reconstruction of the Chee Tor settlement as it may have looked in Romano-British times. This was probably a typical farming settlement of the period, taking advantage of fertile land in the heart of the limestone plateau on a broad shelf above the Wye gorge. There were probably several others in the vicinity, strung out along the valley to take advantage of similar shelves.

by a systematic search for artefacts in the ploughsoil. Extensive excavation to modern standards has not taken place at the sites that are known, with the notable exception of Roystone Grange, hence settlement organisation and agricultural management is not understood in detail. Mixed farming appears to be the norm, with cereals, cattle and sheep. Lead ore and smelting waste at two sites suggests the medieval pattern of farmers supplementing their income by lead mining started in the Roman period. Indeed, the presence of lead ores may have been a critical factor in the location of some of these settlements, although many of the surviving earthwork sites are not in the heart of the ore-rich parts of the limestone plateau, suggesting that agriculture rather than mining was the primary reason for their location.

Complementing the open settlements is a handful of undated enclosures defined by banks, found on the fringes of the highest northern parts of the limestone plateau. These may well be stock pounds for corralling sheep or cattle grazed on the high open pastures of this area. It remains to be tested whether these are Roman or earlier in date.

With the arrival of the Roman armies the Peak District emerges from a period of relative archaeological obscurity, with little as yet known about the Iron Age of the limestone plateau and the shale valleys. The area came under Roman control rapidly and apparently peacefully and a system of forts established, linked by their military roads, to control the mineral resources and the communication routes. The local population prospered in the early years and the evidence suggests that much of the Peak District was given over to farming, with lead mining also being an early contributor to the local economy. Later recession in the Roman Empire sees some impoverishment of the area, flung back onto its own resources at the far reaches of the empire. Following the Roman withdrawal from Britain, the Peak District slides into the poorly understood Dark Ages.

CHAPTER FIVE

From Farm to Village:
Early Medieval Settlement

Names from a distant past: the British after the Romans

Little is known of the British after the Romans departed, nor of the eventual arrival of the first Anglo-Saxons and their new cultural ideas. There are no early documents that illuminate the Dark Age political history of the Peak District and no archaeological sites are known that tell of the general population.

Two pre-Anglian place-names demonstrate the British presence. The name 'Eccles', meaning church, is found both near Hope and Chapel en le Frith. These buildings cannot now be identified. Their presence probably indicates well-established late Roman and post-Roman communities in this part of the Peak. That these people retained their identity for a significant time after the Romans left is suggested by the distribution of other archaeological sites. There is a large number of seventh-century Anglian graves in the Peak District. These concentrate on the limestone plateau and avoid the Hope valley and north-western areas where the Eccles names are found. Between the two is the Grey Ditch at Bradwell. This large linear bank and ditch cuts right across the main valley which provides a route between the Hope valley and the fertile areas of the plateau to the south. There are two other short linear dikes in the region which could also be seen as separating Anglian and British communities.

The British enclave is likely finally to have been fully absorbed into mainstream Anglo-Saxon society with the expansion of the kingdom of Mercia in the eighth century (Figure 26).

The Pecsaete: an Anglian elite and their grave mounds

When Anglian people first entered the Peak District is unknown. Anglian pottery from the ditch surrounding the late Roman 'villa' at Carsington dates to

FIGURE 26 (*opposite*)
Map of the Peak District in Anglian times. The large number of Anglian graves on the limestone plateau, mostly dating from the second half of the seventh century, illustrates the presence of the Pecsaete. In contrast, further north the lack of Anglian graves and the presence of linear earthworks and Eccles place names may well suggest a British enclave.

54

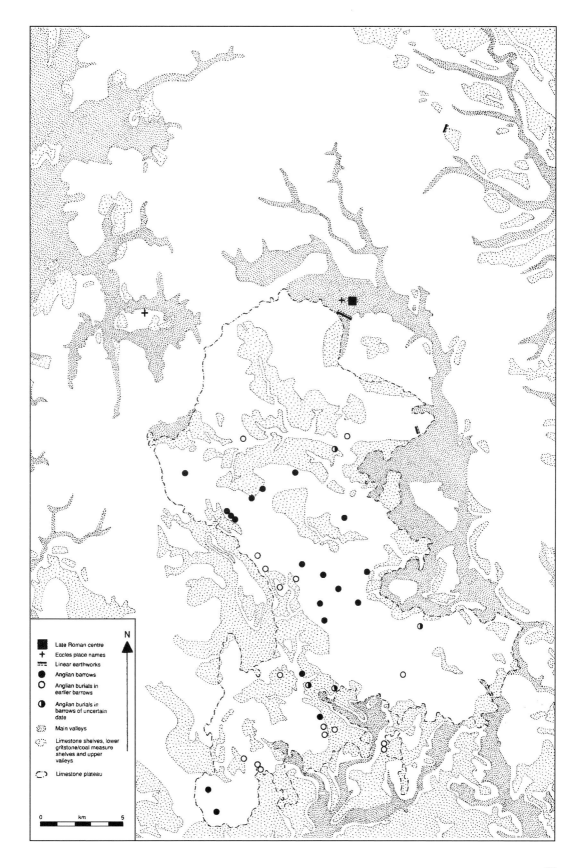

Late Roman centre
Eccles place names
Linear earthworks
Anglian barrows
Anglian burials in earlier barrows
Anglian burials in barrows of uncertain date
Main valleys
Limestone shelves, lower gritstone/coal measure shelves and upper valleys
Limestone plateau

N

0   km   5

the fifth or sixth century. A sixth-century grave is known from a barrow at Musden near Ilam, again at the southern end of the limestone plateau. It seems unlikely that there was wholesale displacement of the British population anywhere in the Peak, but rather a replacement of the British ruling elite with an Anglian one. It is not known if this was through conflict or through inter-marriage with families advocating the new cultural values. Equally we do not know the extent to which the general population was increased, if at all, by incoming Anglian farmers.

In the second half of the seventh-century burial in barrows became relatively common in the region. Thirty-eight burials have definitely been identified while a further twenty four could also date to this period. Some were placed within small earthen mounds built especially, while others were inserted within prehistoric barrows. The bodies were placed in grave pits that were cut east/west, with the head placed west, indicating a Christian rite. The majority were accompanied by grave goods suggesting also a retention of pagan values. These objects were often simple items such as iron knives, but in 15 sites swords, shields, hanging bowls and jewellery in gold, silver and semi-precious stones were buried. One burial from a barrow on Lapwing Hill near Taddington was placed on a bed. With the rich graves at least, these are clearly burials of important members of the local Anglian aristocracy. Even the poorer Peak barrow graves may belong to the warrior elite (Colour Plate 8).

The second half of the seventh century is probably when the *Tribal Hidage* was compiled. This unique document lists all the provinces and client king-doms which paid tribute to the kingdom of Mercia. This identifies the 'Pecsaete', or 'People of the Peak'. Thus, the region was probably a relatively isolated, discrete but well-established entity by this date, surrounded on three sides by bleak gritstone uplands. Uncleared woodlands to the south probably separated it from the Mercian heartlands centred on Repton, Lichfield and Tamworth. The land of the Pecsaete, focused on the limestone plateau and valleys around Bakewell, Matlock, Wirksworth and Ashbourne, was assessed in the Tribal Hidage as having land for 1200 hides, that is lands capable of supporting 1200 families. Thus the population of the region was relatively high. This assessment may well have included the farmers of British stock in the areas under Anglian control and these may have been in the majority.

It is unclear if the Pecsaete were ruled by a dynasty that was politically inde-pendent of Mercia, or whether it had sub-kings imposed by the Mercian House as part of the process of absorption. The kingdom of Mercia had expanded rapidly in the early seventh century, quickly becoming the most powerful kingdom in Britain. In the late seventh century its kings were over-lords of much of southern Britain. The Peak District acted as a useful buffer state along part of its boundary with Northumbria, its main rival. However, by the end of the eighth century, when Mercia had turned its attentions south-wards and westwards, rather than northwards, the kingdom had absorbed all the outlying territories in the Midlands, including the Peak District.

From Farm to Village: Early Medieval Settlement

Symbols in stone: Christian crosses and churches

The conversion of Mercian aristocracy to Christianity began in the second half of the seventh century. The first priests to enter the kingdom were from Northumbria and practised Irish Christianity. However, after the synod of Whitby in 663, the Roman style of worship was generally adopted. By the eighth century the Peak District had been incorporated into the diocese of Lichfield, which helped forge closer political links with the Mercian heartland.

The eighth and early ninth centuries were probably a time of relative stability for the Peak District, even though there may have been continued tension due to the proximity of the Northumbrian border. By now Mercia was well established as one of the most powerful kingdoms of England. Most of its expansionist ambitions were directed against its main rivals, the kingdoms of Wessex and East Anglia, and against the Welsh.

Having largely escaped the earlier ninth-century raids, the problems of the Danes came forcibly to Mercia in the 867, when a Danish army came from York to Nottingham. In 874 King Burgred of Mercia was driven out and fled to Rome, and a large Danish army over-wintered at Repton. In 877 the Danish army returned and began their settlement of the region, retaining political control from that date onwards over much of the northern half of England, in what was to become known as the Danelaw. The lack of distinctive place-names suggests this settlement had only minimal direct impact on the Peak District.

In the early tenth century the political situation again changed, with the territorial expansion of King Edward of Wessex and his sister Aethelflaed, Lady of the Mercians. The Danish borough of Derby fell in 917, followed soon afterwards by the other Danish centres in the north Midlands. One of the final acts of the conquest of Danish Mercia was the building in 920 of a fortified burg at Bakewell, where Edward was accepted as overlord by Danish, English and Scottish leaders from the north. Wessex had finally gained dominance, if still an uneasy one for several decades, and the English kingdom was born.

A surviving bank and ditch defining part of a large oval area in the valley bottom east of the town may be the vestiges of the fortified burg at Bakewell, perhaps occupied only for the short time Edward was here.

The only other identified archaeological structures in the Peak District of later Anglo-Saxon date are a number of crosses and churches. There are two styles of crosses. One of these has been traditionally interpreted as belonging to a flourishing school of Mercian sculpture of the late eighth and early ninth centuries. Crosses at Eyam, Bakewell and Bradbourne churchyards, and tomb-stones at Wirksworth and Bakewell churches, are characterised by ornament such as twisted vine scrolls and by stylised figures. In contrast, there are crosses influenced by Viking art, that have a more severely abstract style with knot-work predominant. These were certainly carved from the late ninth century onwards, and recent reinterpretation of the Mercian-style crosses has proposed that these were also carved at a similar date. The Mercian sculptured pieces

57

are all found at settlements that were probably of above-average importance and are now thought to have been erected as potent symbols of Edward's assertion of authority after 920. In contrast, the Anglo-Danish crosses are not only found at such sites, but also at small settlements and in isolated locations high on the gritstone moorlands. Their precise purpose is unclear. Some may mark boundaries or act as guides to travellers. More examples of Anglo-Saxon sculpture may await discovery; in 1983 parts of two crosses were found amongst rubble in a field close to the site of the now-vanished village of One Ash near Monyash. Bakewell has an unusually large number of carved cross fragments, reused as medieval masonry, all found in the nineteenth century when the church was restored. The town is documented as having a monastery in the mid-tenth century, perhaps founded several decades before. This may explain the large number of crosses (Figure 27).

FIGURE 27

Pre-conquest crosses at Eyam churchyard (left) and Bakewell churchyard (right). These two examples, both now incomplete, illustrate the two styles of carving found in the Peak District. Anglian crosses such as that at Eyam include figurative motifs in the Mercian style and are found at important population centres. Anglo-Danish crosses, as in Bakewell churchyard, have abstract knotwork designs and are found in a variety of locations, sometimes well away from settlements. The Bakewell cross originally stood high on the moors above Darley, near Matlock.

Domesday Book notes six churches that existed before the Norman Conquest. Of these, only Bradbourne has recognisable Anglian fabric, including long and short quoins at the north-east corner of the nave. The churches at Hope, Bakewell, Darley, Wirksworth and Ashbourne appear to have been fully remodelled after the Norman Conquest.

Divisions within the landscape: the emergence of today's villages and their township boundaries

One of the most significant changes in the Peak in recent millennia was the transition from settlements that comprised single farms or small hamlets in the Roman period, to the predominant settlement form of today, the village. This had probably taken place by the time of the Norman Conquest, although new villages continued to be founded on the higher parts of the limestone plateau into the thirteenth century. The process of nucleation is as yet shrouded in mystery but it seems unlikely to be the product of a discontinuity caused by abandonment of the region in the Dark Ages. The many barrow graves of the seventh century suggest an established population. It is equally unlikely to have been the product solely of an increase in population, but was rather the result of abandonment of many small farms combined with the growth of just a few. In some regions of Britain it has been demonstrated that settlements commonly shift site through time, but this seems unlikely for the limestone plateau at least, given the limited number of locations with a reliable water supply. Thus evidence for the more successful early settlements probably lies under the present villages.

Nucleation may well have gone hand in hand with the development of large open fields and the corporate effort needed to make these viable. However, it is equally unclear as to when these fields were first developed, but by analogy with other regions, this is most likely to have been somewhere between the ninth and eleventh centuries. A good case can be made that this process started in the first half of the tenth century in parts of the Peak, with the re-establishment of English control. This appears to go hand in hand with radical social change, with the Crown and manorial lords establishing a firmer power-base by introducing feudal systems of communal tenure, services and obligations.

By the time of the Norman Conquest the present-day pattern of villages had probably largely been established. Only in the north and west did isolated farms remain the norm (see Chapter 7). As Domesday Book illustrates, before the Norman Conquest of 1066 much of the Derbyshire part of the Peak was held by the King and administered through the Royal manors of Hope, Ashford, Bakewell, Darley, Matlock, Wirksworth, Parwich and Ashbourne. Each had a number of berewicks (subsidiary settlements). The survival of these Crown estates and the distinctive way in which they were divided, allows a glimpse of a pattern of land-holding which is perhaps pre-Danish and may date from when the Peak was incorporated into Mercia. There were

probably four main manors, at Hope, Bakewell, Wirksworth and Ashbourne.
Each lies at the heart of one of the four main core areas of population:

Hope	the Hope valley
Bakewell	the eastern limestone shelves and the Wye and Derwent valleys further east
Wirksworth	the south-eastern valleys
Ashbourne	the Dove valley

Although the pattern had fragmented before 1066, with the granting of estates to the Anglo-Saxon aristocracy, each main manor was probably originally subdivided, with subsidiary manors around the fringes. The pattern is difficult to reconstruct in detail. The list given below includes the Royal Manors and privately-held manors which had berewicks in Domesday Book. Bradbourne is also likely to have been important as it has an early-type Anglo-Saxon cross and a pre-Conquest church. Baslow and Hartington are included on topographic grounds to fill gaps in the observed pattern.

Main manors	Other manors	Other possible manors
Hope		Hathersage, Eyam
Bakewell	Ashford, Darley	Baslow, Edensor, Stanton
Wirksworth	Matlock	
Ashbourne	Parwich	Bradbourne, Hartington

The Bakewell manors appear to have had about 12 subsidiary settlements each, which may suggest an artificiality to the listing of berewicks for tax purposes. Thus there may have been further small settlements within the royal manors that were not listed in Domesday Book.

Longdendale, the north-westernmost part of the county, is set apart from the remainder of the county by high gritstone uplands and was an area of small hamlets and farms. This may always have been administered separately.

Alstonefield in Staffordshire may have been the centre of another large, long-standing manor, suggested by fragments of several Anglo-Danish crosses incorporated into the medieval church (Figure 28).

The majority of medieval villages in the Peak District were listed in Domesday Book in 1086. While the names, used here for taxation purposes, may apply to the local administrative land-unit (the township) rather than a dominant village, it may well be that by this date nucleation had taken place

FIGURE 28 (*opposite*)
The organisation of the landscape in late Saxon times. Information in the entries in Domesday Book allows a reconstruction of the pre-Norman landscape. Although parts of the region were in private hands, much was owned by the Crown and divided into eight manors from which it was administered. Each controlled subsidiary villages and hamlets called berewicks. Many of the privately held manors are found in discrete blocks suggesting a systematic division of the region into large manors, perhaps when the region was incorporated into Mercia or later when taken back from Danish control, some of which had subsequently been granted to thanes. The fringe areas of the map are not considered as they relate topographically and administratively to areas beyond the Peak District.

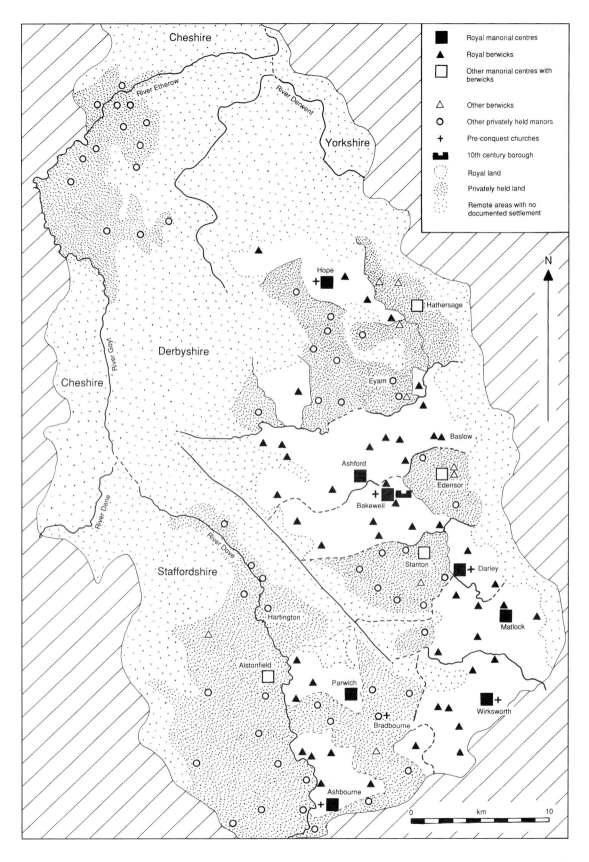

on the Limestone Plateau, in the Derwent Valley, and in the southern valleys. Virtually all of these named settlements still exist and today lie within their own civil parish. By the thirteenth century, when surviving detailed manorial records start to become common, it is clear that feudal villages were the norm here. Over three-quarters of all townships in the Peak District contain a dominant settlement with a name used in 1086. Over large areas there are no further townships, suggesting the pattern of boundaries was well established by this time and may already have been of some antiquity. In the areas where townships now exist that do not correspond to the settlements listed in Domesday Book, several explanations are possible. These areas are mainly in the west and north, where settlement has been more fluid, both because of more severe conditions and because of the tendency for settlement to comprise farms and hamlets rather than villages. The ridges south of Wirksworth also have townships that do not correspond with Domesday settlement and may have been settled later. Elsewhere, there are occasional townships that probably represent subdivision of original boundaries around subsidiary settlement foci, as at Wheston at the edge of Tideswell, and Little Longstone and Wardlow at the edge of Great Longstone. In these cases it is not clear if the subsidiary settlements developed after 1086, or were present then but not mentioned as they were irrelevant for the tax purposes for which Domesday Book was compiled.

CHAPTER SIX

Open Fields, Commons and Waste: Medieval Villages and their Landscape

Domesday Book: A snapshot in time

At the time of Domesday, medieval society was organised in a rigid hierarchy, with the King at the head. William had achieved this by declaring himself the owner of all the land in England at the time of the Conquest and then re-distributing it amongst his nobles. The nobles comprised the lay and ecclesiastical lords, the lesser lords and knights, with freemen below them. Villeins, bordars and cottars made up the next level of society and all were types of bond tenant. Serfs or slaves came at the very base. However, there are no records of there being any freemen, cottars or serfs in the Peak District.

A typical village social structure in the Peak District consisted of the lord of the manor and bond tenants. The latter owed labour services to the lord in return for their land. This usually meant working the demesne lands, the lands held directly by the lord of the manor as well as their own share of the open field held by the villagers.

For the majority of villages of the Peak the first record of their probable presence is Domesday Book. This was compiled in 1086 as a record of the taxable wealth of the English nation. Although many of the settlements, with origins as farms or hamlets, were probably hundreds of years old by this date, earlier detailed records were either never kept or have not survived. Because Domesday Book lists what was taxable, the information it contains needs to be treated with care. For example, such things as the amount of ploughland per village were assessed by a set of formulae which artificially standardised the information. Thus, Domesday Book should be treated not as absolute data, but as a record of relative resources within the region.

The majority of settlements that were untaxable in 1086, classed as waste, concentrate in the north and west. These on the whole were small settlements, topographically and ecologically nearer to being below the threshold of viable subsistence agriculture and thus more prone to abandonment. It may be that some places suffered directly from the military campaigns of William from 1067 to 1070, when he put down resistance to Norman rule in the north.

However, it is more likely that the area as a whole suffered economically due to the instability of the early post-Conquest years. This, and possibly a decrease in population, caused abandonment round the fringes, while richer villages rode the storm more successfully. The distribution of taxable resources reflects differences in geology and topography. The largest ploughlands occur in the sheltered southern valleys with heavy but relatively productive soils. The amount of pasture is greatest on parts of the limestone plateau and southern valleys, while in contrast woodland survived away from the plateau. These woods probably concentrated in the valleys dissecting the gritstone uplands to the north, while to the south-east they would have been found on the steeper slopes within the Derwent valley and on the infertile ridgetops above (Figure 29).

Village and farm: settlement before the Black Death

Most Peak villages still retain their general medieval pattern of layout, even though most buildings are post-medieval in date. Most common, particularly on the limestone plateau, are villages with farms spaced along a single street, with their yards or crofts backing onto the surrounding open field strips. Often the final farms have such names as Townhead or Townend. Classic examples of such layouts are found at Wardlow, Flagg and Chelmorton. Notable exceptions, where village plans are radically different, include the

FIGURE 29 (*opposite*)
The distribution of settlement recorded in Domesday Book, with the amount of arable land, pasture and woodland. All four maps show different distribution patterns which are discussed in the accompanying text. Detailed analyses of entries on amounts of pasture and woodland for individual townships in the region are often divcult, in that figures for the extensive royal manors are given in total but not broken down to specific settlements. Thus, for privately-held manors, where individual details are given, these have been combined into zones of similar size to the royal manors for purposes of analysis. As with Illustration 28, the fringe areas of the region are not considered.

FIGURE 30 (*page 66*)
Examples of medieval village plans in the region. These four examples, drawn from Ordnance Survey maps of *c.*1880, illustrate the variety of village plans that occur. The buildings shown are those present in the late nineteenth century. However only those boundaries which appear to reflect the medieval layout are drawn. Castleton is a rare example of a planned settlement, laid out below Peveril Castle, within its own town earthworks and including a market place with adjacent church. Monyash was also a place of more than average importance. It again had a market place, now partly infilled, which grew up adjacent to the natural ponds that allowed large numbers of stock to be watered. Today it no longer has a market and is no larger than many surrounding villages; medieval house platforms can be identified between the present buildings and there is a banked enclosure of unknown function to the west. Wardlow is typical of the commonest village pattern, which comprises a single street with farms spaced along it. Warslow has a nucleated non-linear plan, in this case defined by an unusual series of sunken lanes.

FIGURE 31 (*page 67*)
Map of the Peak District in medieval times. Much of the limestone plateau and the surrounding main valleys were extensively settled, with villages surrounded by open fields in the traditional settlement zones. However, around the high fringes of the region, settlement was more dispersed and these areas were the focus for hunting forests, mostly belonging to the Crown. The Norman manorial centres tend to be where early castles and churches were built. Many more churches were built in the twelfth to thirteenth centuries and market centres were formalised by charter at this time.

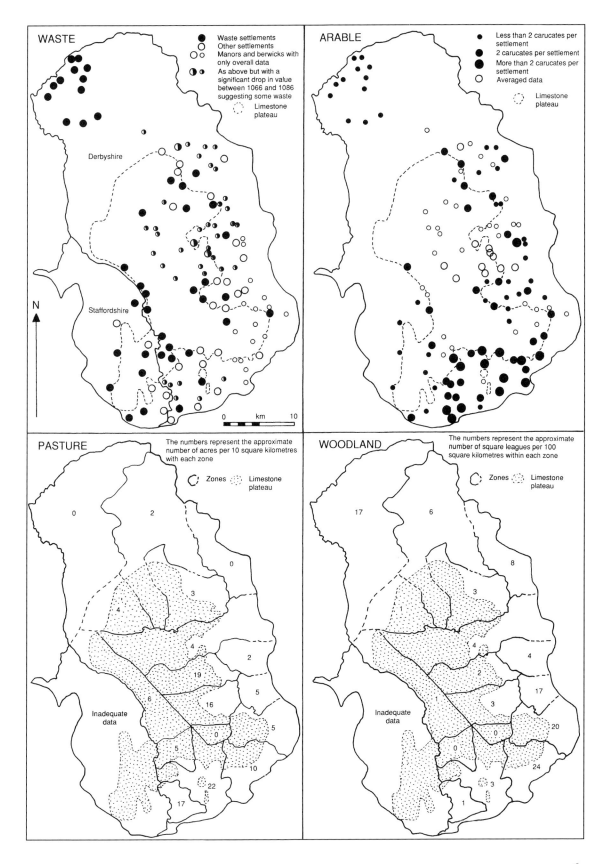

WASTE

- ● Waste settlements
- ○ Other settlements
- ○○ Manors and berwicks with only overall data
- ◐ ◑ As above but with a significant drop in value between 1066 and 1086 suggesting some waste
- ⦿ Limestone plateau

Derbyshire

Staffordshire

N

0   km   10

ARABLE

- ● Less than 2 carucates per settlement
- ● 2 carucates per settlement
- ● More than 2 carucates per settlement
- ○ Averaged data
- ⦿ Limestone plateau

PASTURE

The numbers represent the approximate number of acres per 10 square kilometres with each zone

Zones ⦿ Limestone plateau

Inadequate data

0   2
0
3
4
4
4
2
19
5
6   16
0
5
5
5
10
22
17

WOODLAND

The numbers represent the approximate number of square leagues per 100 square kilometres within each zone

Zones ⦿ Limestone plateau

Inadequate data

17   6
8
3
1   4
4
2   4
1   17
3
1   3   20
0
0   24
1   3
1

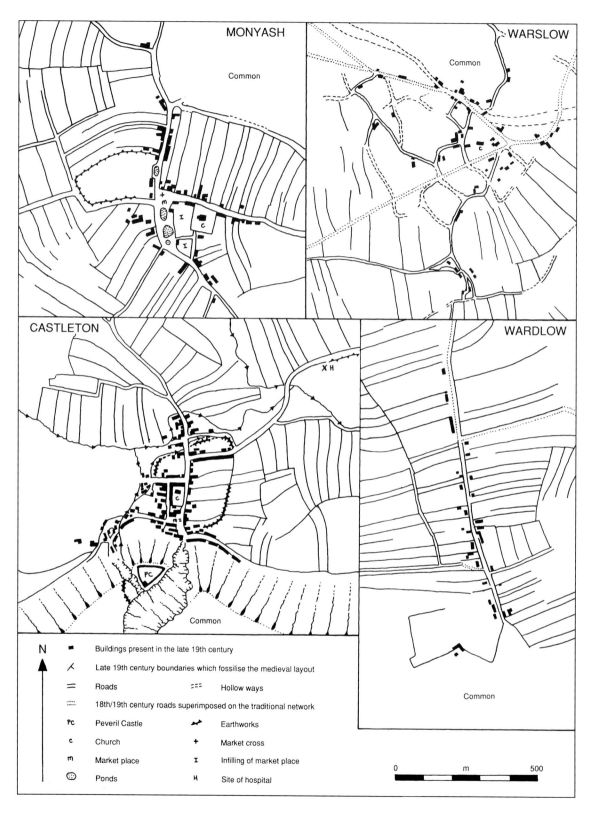

MONYASH

WARSLOW

Common

Common

c

CASTLETON

WARDLOW

X H

c

PC

Common

Common

N

- Buildings present in the late 19th century

✗ Late 19th century boundaries which fossilise the medieval layout

= Roads   ┅ Hollow ways

⁖ 18th/19th century roads superimposed on the traditional network

PC Peveril Castle   ➶ Earthworks

c Church   + Market cross

m Market place   I Infilling of market place

⊙ Ponds   H Site of hospital

0   m   500

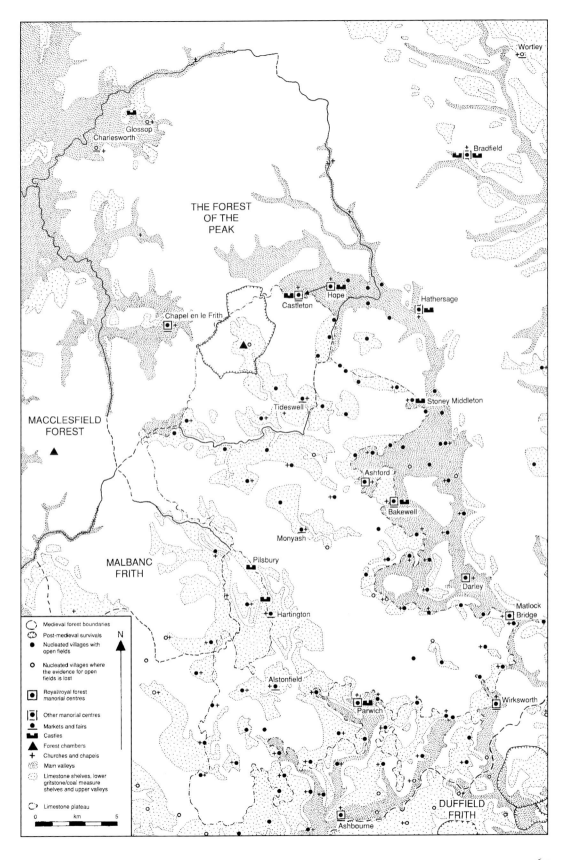

THE FOREST
OF THE
PEAK

Wortley

Glossop
Charlesworth

Bradfield

Chapel en le Frith

Castleton
Hope

Hathersage

Stoney Middleton

MACCLESFIELD
FOREST

Tideswell

Ashford

Bakewell

Monyash

MALBANC
FRITH

Pilsbury

Darley

Matlock
Bridge

Hartington

Medieval forest boundaries

Post-medieval survivals

Nucleated villages with
open fields

Nucleated villages where
the evidence for open
fields is lost

Royal/royal forest
manorial centres

Other manorial centres

Markets and fairs

Castles

Forest chambers

Churches and chapels

Main valleys

Limestone shelves, lower
gritstone/coal measure
shelves and upper valleys

Limestone plateau

N

Alstonfield

Parwich

Wirksworth

DUFFIELD
FRITH

Ashbourne

0   km   5

planned market settlement of Castleton below Peveril Castle, and other villages built round market places, such as at Monyash, Tideswell, Hartington and Alstonefield. Other village patterns, such as Warslow, Beeley and Ashford, are also atypical but why is not yet clear (Figures 30, 31).

Not all of the Peak District was dominated by villages in the medieval period. To the north and west particularly, but also along the shelves flanking the eastern gritstone moors and on the ridges to the south-east, farming was predominantly undertaken from scattered farms and hamlets. Although documentation of these small settlements often exists, their medieval layout is obscured by later buildings. Whenever a dwelling was rebuilt, whether at an isolated farm or in a village, a building range was either extended or a new site was chosen in order that the old house could be used until the new was completed. Old dwellings were then demolished or used as outbuildings. Thus, through time, farms change plan, and buildings change function (Figure 32).

Several medieval villages have been abandoned. Domesday Book records a handful of settlements, such as Muchedeswell, Waterfield and Soham, whose sites were lost at an early date, either abandoned, shifted or renamed. Other sites which have surviving earthworks were abandoned in late medieval or subsequent times, for example Nether Haddon, Conksbury, Smerrill and Lea Hall. Here there are hollow-ways, low platforms marking the sites of rectangular timber buildings, and banks defining yards. These deserted medieval villages are small compared with many examples found further south in the clay vales of the Midlands. Several villages in the Peak have shrunk rather than become completely deserted, with house platforms in open plots between the present buildings. While some of these were always quite small settlements, as at Ballidon and Blackwell, there are others such as Monyash which were once more important centres (Figures 33, 34).

Open fields and walled closes: farming before the Black Death

In the medieval period, the limestone plateau, with the exception of some of the most isolated areas to north and west, was a landscape containing villages surrounded by large open fields. These fields are likely to have evolved along with the feudal system of land holding, which in this region may well have been in place by the Norman Conquest, probably first developed in the early tenth century. Superficially at least, the fields are typical of those common to the clay vales of the Midlands. Each plateau village was surrounded by a large coherent area of open fields. These incorporated access lanes running between parcels or furlongs, each of many long thin strips, which were variously

FIGURE 32 (*opposite*)
Map showing medieval settlement zones in the Peak District. The central part of the region is dominated by nucleated villages surrounded by open fields. In the higher parts of this zone monastic granges also existed. To the north and west settlement was generally dispersed comprising hamlets and single farms. Only a few of the hamlets are known to have small open fields. Between the two zones and to the east, there is a zone where both settlement types mix.

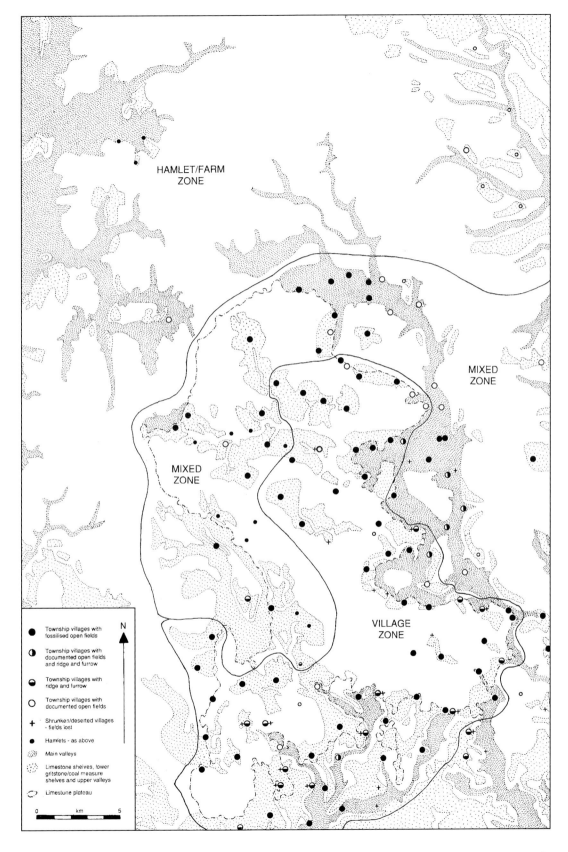

HAMLET/FARM
ZONE

MIXED
ZONE

MIXED
ZONE

VILLAGE
ZONE

N

	Township villages with fossilised open fields
	Township villages with documented open fields and ridge and furrow
	Township villages with ridge and furrow
	Township villages with documented open fields
+	Shrunken/deserted villages - fields lost
•	Hamlets - as above
	Main valleys
	Limestone shelves, lower gritstone/coal measure shelves and upper valleys
	Limestone plateau

0   km   5

69

FIGURE 33
Nether Haddon deserted medieval village. The main hollow way can be seen winding its way up the slope from left to right with the rectangular crofts to either side. Beyond the village are the extensive remains of the ridge and furrow and lynchets of the medieval field system. To the bottom left is the early seventeenth-century dovecote of Haddon Hall. Among the village earthworks can be seen several oval mounds; these are artificial rabbit warrens, known as pillow mounds, built after the village was abandoned to keep the hall well supplied with rabbits for the table.

oriented, usually taking account of the topography. The partition of land into strips enabled it to be divided between the lord and his farmers, each getting a share of rich and poor land. Without hedges or walls between strips the fields were worked communally where necessary. The presence of the strips in itself is a strong indicator that arable farming was important at this time. However, given that the Peak is an upland area, it seems likely that livestock were always of greater economic importance than crop cultivation, even during the twelfth to thirteenth centuries when open field farming was at its height. Thus, although the trend to enclose strips is traditionally seen as starting in the fourteenth century, corresponding with decline in both climate and population,

FIGURE 34
A reconstruction of how Nether Haddon village may have looked in medieval times.

the possibility cannot be discounted that enclosure of some strips to form permanent pastures, particularly where land was poor, may have taken place earlier, perhaps almost from the outset. In some cases, there were probably open outfields that were only used occasionally, when greater cropping capacity became desirable. Probable evidence for this practice has recently been identified above Edensor, within what later became Chatsworth Park. Some of these at least may well have fallen totally out of use in the fourteenth century and were never enclosed.

Unenclosed land beyond the open fields was mostly used as common pasture. In the case of higher land this may have been rough grazing dominated by coarse grasses and heather. Such areas were used as sources of peat and turf. On the limestone plateau, the steep dry-valleys and limestone gorges are the most likely sources of timber and brushwood and some at least may have remained thickly wooded throughout the medieval period (Figure 35).

Throughout the higher areas of the limestone plateau and in other relatively remote areas of the region, mostly on the upper fringes of established settlement, there was a scatter of medieval farms, called granges. These were owned and run by monasteries sited throughout the Midlands. In some cases the granges were built alongside or supplanted earlier settlement, as at One Ash which is listed in Domesday Book. More commonly they appear to be at new sites. The majority are very poorly documented and there may well have been others that await discovery. Records, as far as they allow, suggest foundation dates commonly in the twelfth and thirteenth centuries. These granges have traditionally been thought of as sheep farms and in many cases this was undoubtedly true. Well over half belonged to Cistercian abbeys, an order well known for its involvement in the wool trade. However, sheep farming was not the only activity, as demonstrated by examples such as Needham Grange, north of Hartington, again a Cistercian grange, which has fossilised open-field strip boundaries associated with it. From the fourteenth century onwards many of the granges, due to climatic decline and political unrest, may well have been less profitable concerns than they had been previously. Indeed, in common with practices across Britain in the fourteenth and fifteenth centuries, many of the granges were leased to lay tenants (Figure 36).

In a few instances surviving wall foundations of grange buildings have been identified. Excavations have taken place at Roystone Grange near Ballidon and at probable grange buildings at Blackwell (see Figure 48). Around several granges there are remains of boundary earthworks. These are particularly extensive on the high limestone plateau above the Dove valley (Figure 37).

In the various Peak landscapes beyond the limestone plateau medieval farming changed according to topography. The southern valleys were again a zone of villages and open fields. The Derwent valley had a mixture of villages with open fields along the valley bottom, and hamlets and farms in more isolated locations, such as in steeper wooded areas and on gritstone shelves high above the valley. In northern and western parts of the Peak District,

FIGURE 35 (*opposite*)
Medieval open fields and commons in the heart of the limestone plateau. This map shows a typical example of medieval land division in the more fertile parts of the plateau. Large open fields surrounded villages, while steep dale-sides and upper land was open common or waste. From the fourteenth century onwards, if not before, the open fields began to be enclosed, fossilising the cultivation strip pattern and thus allowing it to be reconstructed today. Abbey granges at One Ash and Calling Low to the south-east had been divided into large rectangular fields by the early seventeenth century, the date of the earliest cartographic evidence for these properties. One Ash was mentioned in Domesday Book prior to its becoming a grange. At some point before the seventeenth century it changed site to a more-sheltered location to the north-east. The commons, which were used for open grazing, were not enclosed until the second half of the eighteenth century and the beginning of the nineteenth century. They were a valuable source of resources such as timber and brushwood. Medieval documents also illustrate that rights of turbary were disputed, which indicates that peat and turf were being cut.

FIGURE 36 (*page 74*)
Monastic granges in the Peak District and their mother houses. Abbeys and priories spread over much of the Midlands held land in the Peak District. Over 50 granges are known to have existed, many of which are still farms today.

FIGURE 37 (*page 75*)
Medieval granges above Pilsbury and the River Dove, north of Hartington. Good examples of boundaries associated with medieval granges can be identified at Cronkstone, Needham, Pilsbury and Cotesfield, together with hamlets at Pilsbury and Hurdlow. Three of the granges belonged to the Cistercian abbey at Merevale in Warwickshire. The exception was Cotesfield, which was the property of the Cistercian Combermere Abbey in Cheshire. The enclosed areas around the granges were sometimes used for arable as well as for pasture, as indicated by the reverse-S strip fields at Needham. The outfields and unenclosed commons beyond were presumably extensively used for the sheep flocks. The lead mining respected by the boundary of Cotesfield provides a rare example of a site where medieval or earlier mining can be demonstrated.

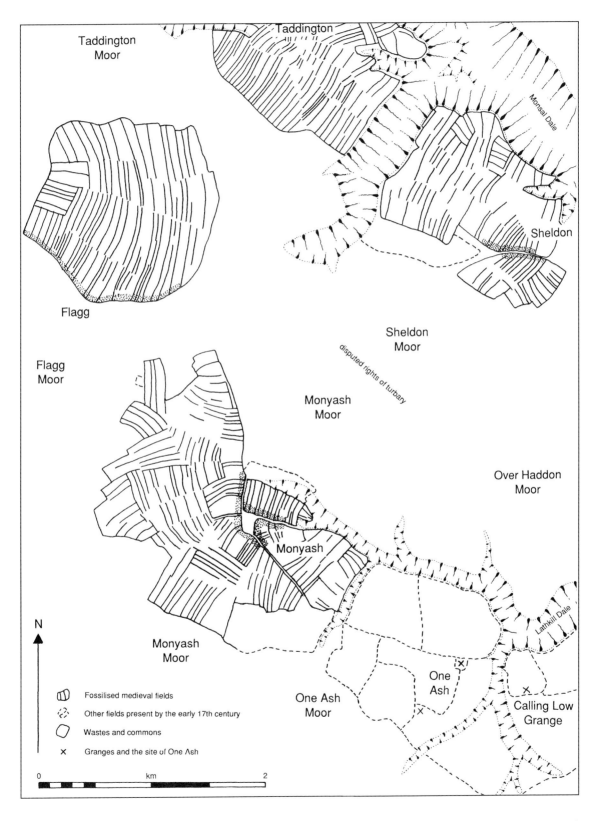

Taddington
Moor

Taddington

Monsal Dale

Sheldon

Flagg

Sheldon
Moor

Flagg
Moor

disputed rights of turbary

Monyash
Moor

Over Haddon
Moor

Monyash

Lathkill Dale

N

Monyash
Moor

One
Ash

One Ash
Moor

Calling Low
Grange

Fossilised medieval fields

Other fields present by the early 17th century

Wastes and commons

×   Granges and the site of One Ash

0   km   2

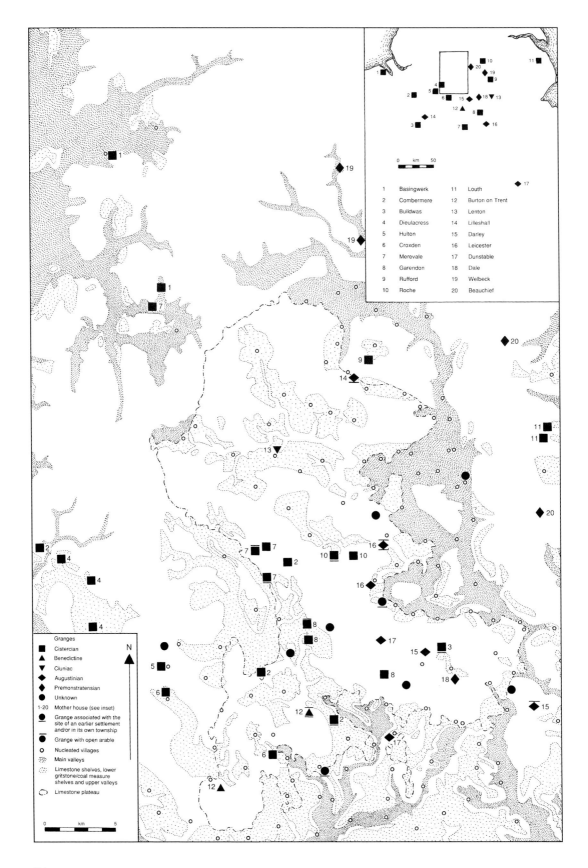

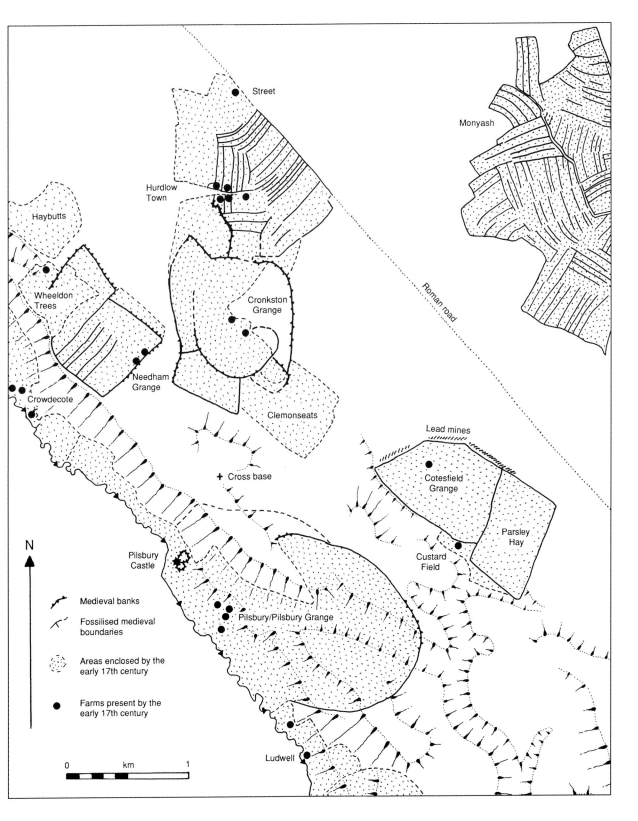

Street

Monyash

Hurdlow
Town

Haybutts

Wheeldon
Trees

Cronkston
Grange

Needham
Grange

Crowdecote

Clemonseats

Lead mines

+ Cross base

Cotesfield
Grange

Parsley
Hay

Custard
Field

Pilsbury
Castle

N

Pilsbury/Pilsbury Grange

Medieval banks

Fossilised medieval
boundaries

Areas enclosed by the
early 17th century

Farms present by the
early 17th century

Ludwell

Roman road

0   km   1

farms and hamlets predominated. High gritstone uplands everywhere remained unoccupied.

It is unclear how the medieval landscape was divided when farmed from hamlets and farms rather than villages. With the medieval granges of the limestone plateau, like those above the River Dove and at Roystone Grange, the impression from surviving boundaries is that large pastures and arable areas were defined by boundary banks or walls, but that these were not sub-divided into walled or hedged closes or yards, except within small areas in the vicinity of the farm buildings. In a few cases there were certainly small strip fields. Fossilised examples can occasionally be identified, for example in the northwest at some of the hamlets around Glossop. In addition, open fields have been documented at several hamlets in the north-east around Bradfield. A similar picture is gained from the isolated enclosure on the gritstone moors at Lawrence Field, above Hathersage. In contrast with the picture just presented, by the early seventeenth century many favourable areas beyond the medieval open fields had been enclosed into large rectangular, or smaller irregularly shaped, walled or hedged fields. This is demonstrated by the surveys undertaken by William Senior of the Cavendish holdings scattered across the region, the earliest extensive cartographic evidence for the region to show field boundaries. While some of these fields may have been created in the sixteenth century, with improvement resulting from a change of ownership after the acquisition of monastic estates at the Dissolution, in some cases they may be much earlier. In some areas away from the limestone plateau, the possibility that areas of small irregular walled fields still in use today have origins in later prehistory should not be ruled out (Figures 38, 39).

From cereals to sheep: changes in farming practice in later medieval times

In the fourteenth century Britain was hit by a series of disasters. In the first decades of the century there was the onset of colder and wetter climatic conditions, which had a marked affect on crop yields leading to famines. In 1348–49 the Black Death devastated the country, killing over a third of population. These factors bred social and political unrest, the later medieval period being one of endemic warfare, which continued until radical resolution in the sixteenth century, with the Reformation and beginnings of Renaissance under the Tudors.

The plague does not appear to have had much impact in the Peak District. Depopulation was probably the result of people moving to better lowland areas which needed new blood after having suffered from the plague. Others were forced off the land as landlords increased their sheep flocks.

With population decrease and reduced crop yields in the Peak, the traditional feudal system of open field agriculture became unworkable and the emphasis moved strongly towards livestock, particularly sheep, although smaller parcels of open strip fields were retained. At this time, if not before, significant parts of the open fields started to be enclosed as stock pastures.

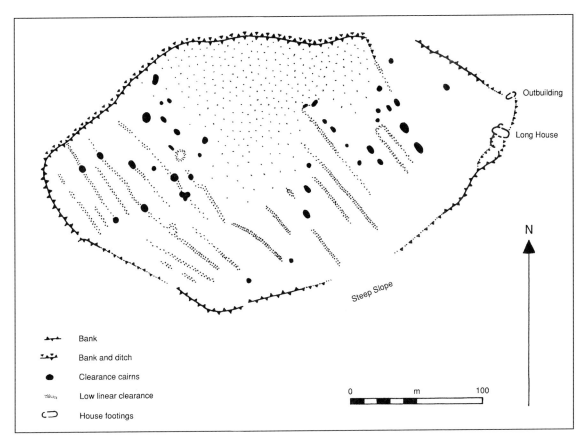

Bank

Bank and ditch

Clearance cairns

Low linear clearance

House footings

0   m   100

N

Outbuilding

Long House

Steep Slope

FIGURE 38

The Lawrence Field enclosure above Hathersage. This small upland farm, sited in relative isolation on a south-east facing gritstone shelf, was carved out of moorland common in the medieval period. The infield is defined by a low bank and ditch and was used for arable, as indicated by the narrow cleared strips and clearance cairns, except in a small portion to the north which was too stony to cultivate. In the eastern corner are two buildings and a yard, the larger building probably a dwelling and byre, the other an outhouse. Unpublished excavations in the mid-twentieth century produced pottery believed to be of eleventh- to twelfth-century date.

Where this happened it appears smaller individual parcels were often allocated permanently to specific farmers, while larger areas were used for shared grazing. Even today many village farm holdings retain small parcels scattered across what were once open fields, reflecting their permanent subdivision from later medieval times onwards. Many small individual parcels containing only a few strips were eventually walled out, thus fossilising the original strip layout. This enclosure happened piecemeal over a long period. By the time of the Enclosure Awards of the late eighteenth and early nineteenth centuries, there were often still areas of open strips surviving. Frequently these parcels represented only a small percentage of the original open field extent, but occasionally over half the original field was still farmed in the traditional way, a notable example being at Bakewell where large areas of open field survived until the early nineteenth century.

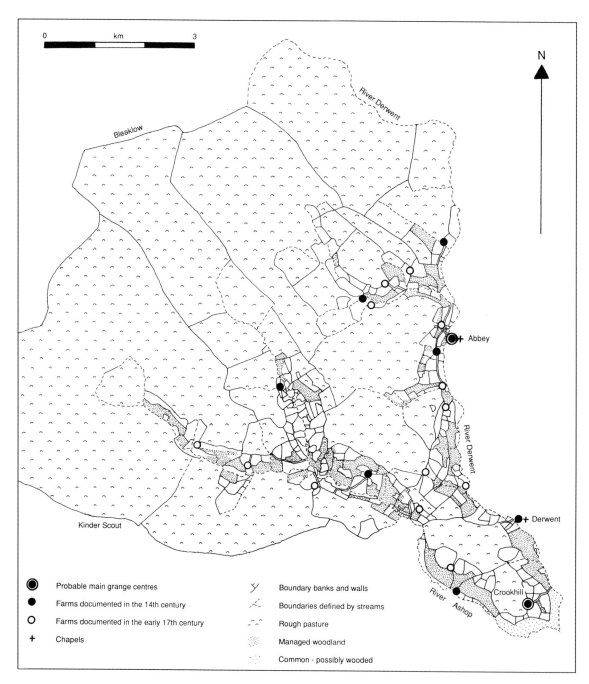

FIGURE 39

Single farms in the Upper Derwent valley and its tributaries. William Senior undertook surveys in 1627 for the Cavendish family at Chatsworth, who owned all the land west of the Derwent. The farming pattern east of the Derwent cannot be reconstructed in the same detail, due to the lack of early cartographic data. In the early thirteenth century the whole Upper Derwent area was granted to the Premonstratensian monks of Welbeck Abbey in Nottinghamshire, who appear to have had two main granges in the valley. They held the land until the Dissolution. The extent and nature of medieval enclosure throughout the valley may well have been similar to the seventeenth century, as documentation shows that many of the farms in the valley existed by the fourteenth century.

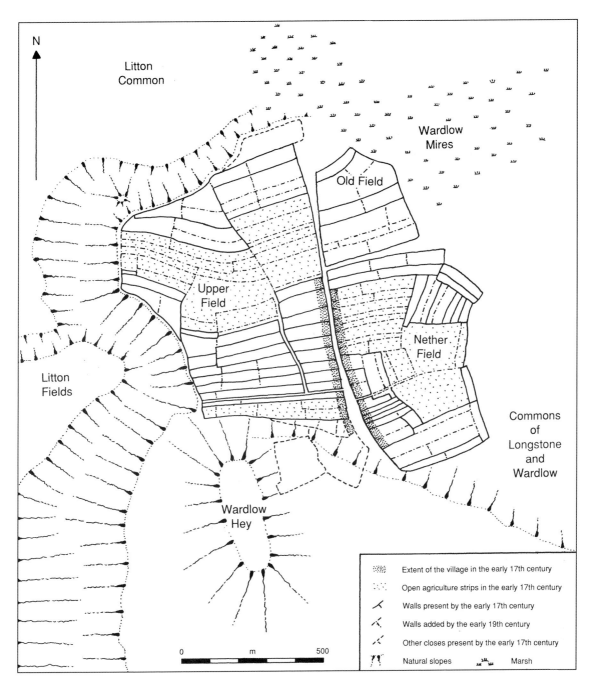

N

Litton
Common

Wardlow
Mires

Old Field

Upper
Field

Nether
Field

Litton
Fields

Commons
of
Longstone
and
Wardlow

Wardlow
Hey

Extent of the village in the early 17th century	
Open agriculture strips in the early 17th century	
Walls present by the early 17th century	
Walls added by the early 19th century	
Other closes present by the early 17th century	
Natural slopes	Marsh

0   m   500

FIGURE 40

The fossilised medieval field system at Wardlow. At this small one-street village, between Tideswell and Eyam, the full extent of its medieval open fields can be reconstructed, as the cultivation strips have been fossilised by narrow walled fields. The first detailed cartographic evidence for the parish is a fine survey by William Senior drawn in 1617 for the Cavendish family, who owned the township at that date. By this time well over half of the open fields had been enclosed.

FIGURE 41
Ridge and furrow around Tissington. In the heavy clay soils on the southern and to a lesser extent eastern fringes of the limestone plateau, large expanses of broad ridge and furrow survive, which reflect the medieval pattern of cultivation. However, the strips were often still in use, and being modified in some cases, well into the post-medieval period.

On the limestone plateau, villages today are typically surrounded by distinctive thin fields fossilising much or all of the medieval open field. There are many fine examples, at Chelmorton, Flagg, Monyash and Wardlow, and these distinctive walled areas are one of the dominant features of the present landscape. They are defined by many miles of walls, whose origins range from the medieval period to the nineteenth century. However, normally no difference can be perceived between early and late walls. Even if methods of construction have changed, walls are continually falling down and being rebuilt or repaired, hence differences are masked. The process of development of enclosure within open fields is therefore hard to unravel unless early parish or estate maps are available (Figure 40; Colour Plate 9).

Beyond the limestone plateau the pattern of open field fossilisation is less complete. In rare cases, as at Longnor, there are coherent areas of walled strips. More commonly, in the shale valleys, hedges partly define the medieval pattern. Hedges are easier to move than walls, leading to the increased fragmentation. However, in these valleys, and on limestone-shale shelves around the fringes of the limestone plateau, medieval-type cultivation strips can commonly still be seen within later rectangular fields. Because there are relatively deep heavy soils here, ridge and furrow development is good. This is most common on the southern fringes of the Peak, round villages such as Tissington and Bradbourne, where whole swathes of land are covered by the prominent corrugation of parallel ridges. Exceptional cases exist elsewhere in the Peak in Chatsworth Park and on Haddon Fields west of Haddon Hall. Emparkment in one case and depopulation in the other, has led to fossilisation of these two arable landscapes at relatively early dates. Fine ridge and furrow, and strip lynchets, also exists west of Bakewell, where late enclosure and later non-intensive farming by a large number of smallholders has led to good survival (Figures 41, 50).

In contrast to the shale landscapes, medieval ridge and furrow is rarely found on the thin soils of the limestone plateau. The only notable exceptions are on steep slopes, where strips have been terraced into hillsides, as at Priestcliffe where prominent lynchetted terraces are visible from the A6.

Not all ridge and furrow is of medieval date. Typical medieval ridge and furrow is broad and somewhat sinuous. Straight and often narrow ridge and furrow is often post-medieval in date. However, these are over-simplifications. Much of the medieval type continued to be ploughed into the seventeenth and eighteenth centuries wherever traditional strips continued in use. Not all ridge and furrow is created by the plough, some being hand dug. Examples of hand dug broad ridges are known in the region that may be as early as Roman in date.

Even on the limestone plateau, not all parishes have fossilised medieval fields. Where villages had been radically depopulated and later farmed by a single landowner, wholesale division of the former open fields into large rectangular fields eventually took place. Brushfield is a classic example.

CHAPTER SEVEN

The Walled Landscape: Post-Medieval Farming and Enclosure

Closes and enclosures: contrasting field patterns

Much of the Peak District is an enclosed landscape dominated by drystone walls, with the exception of the open moorland of the higher gritstone uplands. The field boundaries defining fossilised medieval open fields are discussed above. Beyond these, the walls which divide the surrounding landscape into rectangular fields are largely a product of enclosure from the sixteenth to nineteenth centuries. Many farmsteads were built during this period, set amongst new intakes taken in from moor and common, often in areas that previously had been almost exclusively farmed from nucleated villages. Much of the land that was enclosed was common land and this led to disenfranchisement of most of the poorer people of the region. Today the Peak District has one of the smallest percentages of common land in the country.

The conventional model for post-medieval enclosure is that private piecemeal enclosure is early and the fields are small. This is contrasted with eighteenth- and nineteenth-century fields, laid out at the time of parish Enclosure Awards, where agreement to enclose was reached through Acts of Parliament. Such fields are characterised by being large, with ruler-straight boundaries which were drawn on maps before being built. This model is over-simplistic for the Peak District (Figure 42).

Irrespective of date, field size is probably determined by the number of people with a claim on land in any given parish. Some limestone-plateau villages in particular had high populations, and smaller farms were viable here because occupiers had a second income from lead-mining. Around Elton and Winster, for example, many mines existed and the enclosures, laid out in the eighteenth century, are typically small. Conversely, many large fields were laid out at an early date, as illustrated by the Senior surveys of the early seventeenth century. At One Ash and Meadow Place, east of Monyash for example (see Figure 35), large fields were only subdivided in the eighteenth and nineteenth centuries, to bring them into line with fashionable contemporary farming practice. In Castleton parish, there is a rare survival of the map for a late seventeenth-century private enclosure agreement. This divides the common into large fields with ruler-straight boundaries.

FIGURE 42

Field patterns around Monyash. This aerial view illustrates the still often narrow strip field enclosure in the foreground and centre, which took place in piecemeal fashion. This contrasts with that beyond the village which was planned later, at the time of the Monyash Enclosure Award of 1776. This is characterised by boundaries drawn ruler-straight on maps before being built on the ground.

About half the parishes of the Peak had a Parliamentary Enclosure Award, ranging in date from the mid-eighteenth to mid-nineteenth century. Often large areas of upland common were enclosed, the lower land having already long been divided into fields. A typical example is Monyash, where the medieval open field was already fully enclosed. The whole parish beyond this was divided into large fields in the 1770s. In contrast, in the 1820s' Award for Tideswell and Wheston, while some areas of common were divided into relatively large fields, other parts were divided into particularly small fields. This

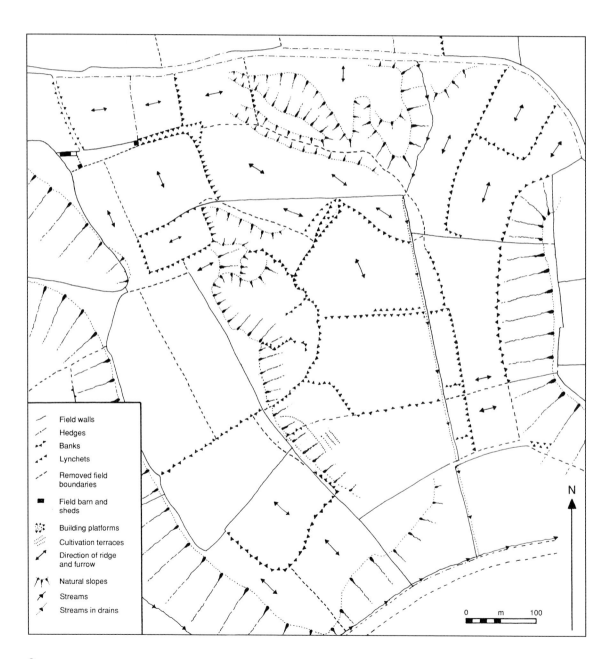

Field walls
Hedges
Banks
Lynchets
Removed field
boundaries
Field barn and
sheds
Building platforms
Cultivation terraces
Direction of ridge
and furrow
Natural slopes
Streams
Streams in drains

0   m   100

N

presumably reflects the large population of Tideswell, which was a market centre with many service trades as well as a farming community.

Large private improvement schemes also took place in the eighteenth and nineteenth centuries, undertaken by large estates such as that of the dukes of Devonshire at Chatsworth. In these cases earlier fields were swept away, in contrast with elsewhere, where relatively poor farmers normally modified older fields in piecemeal fashion. Moorland was also taken in, as at Rodknoll on East Moor, south-east of Baslow, where over two square kilometres of land was covered with a chequerboard of near-identical rectangular fields. These estate farms sometimes mirror examples in contemporary books on fashionable farming practice. This includes such details as gates that cut field corners diagonally. Land belonging to estates is also characterised by extravagances such as plantations sited primarily to be decorative as well as being long-term investments within the landscape (Figure 43).

Stone and water: walls, field kilns and dew ponds

The fields of the Peak District commonly contain minor agricultural features which add character to the region, but which unfortunately are now disappearing as they have become redundant. Field walls themselves can be informative. Detailed study at Roystone Grange, near Ballidon, has shown that early walls can be identified partly by the large vertically-set stones at their bases, even though the upper parts may well have been rebuilt several times. However, it is not clear how widely this observation can be applied, even in the Peak. The use of large orthostats may well reflect initial clearance of land and the use of surface boulders, irrespective of period. There are walls near Baslow, for example, that have orthostats which are known to date from post-medieval times. Conversely, medieval walls fossilising cultivation strips within open fields are unlikely to have orthostats, because these areas had previously been used for agriculture (Figure 44).

Wall furniture can also be informative and unfortunately these features are often not replaced when walls are rebuilt. Few gates still have both their stone posts as they were set too close together for modern equipment. Gritstone posts, which were easy to dress, sometimes have a variety of slots and holes showing they were once closed by wooden bars rather than hinged gates. Sheep throughs or creeps, low gaps with stone lintels to allow the passage of sheep, show the fields were used for sheep grazing. Occasionally, in areas near Sheffield, there are blocks of fields which never had throughs. These were laid out in the nineteenth century especially for cattle, reflecting the increased importance of dairying to service the needs of the growing city. There are two

FIGURE 43 (*opposite*)
An agricultural landscape between Bubnell and Hassop fossilised around the turn of the twentieth century. Many of the present fields were laid out between 1879 and 1919 when Chatsworth Estate, which owns this land, decided radically to reorganise it to make larger fields that were easier to manage. Much of this land has not subsequently been ploughed, leaving ridge and furrow and the boundary earthworks of the previous field pattern clearly visible.

Romano-British	Medieval
Elevation	Elevation
Section Foundation plan	Section Foundation plan
16th Century Onwards	**19th Century**
Elevation Section Foundation plan	Elevation Section Foundation plan

The Peak District: Landscapes Through Time

FIGURE 44
Roystone Grange: walls through the ages. Detailed recording of the walls around Roystone Grange, near Ballidon, together with selected small excavations, have shown that wall building styles here changed through time. In earlier periods, when there was much surface stone to be cleared off the land, large stones were used at the bases of walls, set in double rows in the Romano-British period, perhaps surmounted by earthen banks, and single rows in the medieval period. By the sixteenth century walls were exclusively built of smaller material, but this was still surface gathered. The most common wall type is of nineteenth-century date, which in contrast was built of angular stone quarried nearby. While recent work at Roystone suggests this model of development may be over-simplistic, it may be that the general pattern holds true.

PLATE 2 (*opposite*)
The interior of Arbor Low from the crest of the barrow superimposed on the henge bank. This site, south of Monyash, although relatively well preserved, looks very different from how it did in prehistory. The most obvious change is that nearly all the stones have fallen or have been pulled down. Close inspection of the ring of stones reveals one stone that has not fully fallen, several vertically set stumps, one with the broken top adjacent, and several shattered stones that broke when they hit the ground. Several stones have been removed from the site, one of which until recently lay against a wall next to the path up to the site. One of the stones in the ring has only been partly removed, the remaining portion having a drill hole visible, made to split the stone.

The Five Wells chambered cairn. One of the internal chambers of this stone-built mound on Taddington Moor. This was exposed when the mound was partly removed by wall builders about 200 years ago. It had its capstone broken up and removed, but the massive side slabs remain. The tomb is located on the false crest of one of the most prominent ridges of the limestone plateau, high above the Wye valley gorge and fertile shelves to either side. It is carefully sited to have extensive views over this land, an area presumably widely used by the people who built the monument. Thus the Earlier Neolithic herders were overlooked by their ancestors, while at the same time the mound was obvious in the landscape when first constructed, because it was built of white limestone. In such ways traditional tenure over the land could be maintained and strengthened.

PLATE 3
The Arbor Low henge as it may have looked in prehistory. This reconstruction shows the monument at a developed stage of its life. The first feature to be built was probably the bank, made from material from the inner quarry ditch. When first built the bank may well have been intended to be seen as an eye-catching feature of white limestone, mixed with orange clay. The earthworks may have surrounded features built of timber, perhaps free-standing rings of posts and possibly roofed buildings. At other henges in Britain, more extensively excavated than Arbor Low, the trend was for timber features to be rebuilt in stone, sometimes when the site was already hundreds of years old. At Arbor Low neither the stone circle nor the central features could be seen from outside the monument, except through its entrances. The two massive slabs of the cove at the heart of the site prevented any rituals carried out here from being visible even through the entrances. Thus strangers were excluded from seeing these. Many tribal members allowed within the monument, while participating in much that happened, probably played a passive role when observing what took place in the cove. This area may have been the preserve of shamen or other leaders. The henge continued to be used in the Bronze Age, at which time a community laid claim to it in a dramatic way, by the demolition of part of the outer bank to build a large round barrow on the line of the bank. A similar barrow was superimposed on the Gib Hill long barrow just visible in the background to the right.

PLATE 4
The Bull Stone near Wincle. This highly unusual and little-known site is unparalleled elsewhere in the Peak District. The central standing stone is encircled by a low ring of closely-spaced stones at the edge of what appears to be a flat-topped platform. This site does not fit easily within the usual descriptive categories for prehistoric monuments and

highlights the danger of straight-jacketing our interpretations. While the low mound may suggest there are burials here and that this is an unusual form of barrow, the focal point is the central stone. The site is similar to a number of stone circles in south-western Scotland with tall central stones with surrounding rings of sometimes small but spaced stones. Why a site of this design was built in the Peak District remains a mystery.

PLATE 5
A selection of the grave-goods from Liffs Low barrow near Biggin. These include two fine flint axes (left), an unusual pottery flask and flint tools (centre), and an antler macehead, two boar's tusk knives and two pieces of red ochre (right).

PLATE 6
One of the urns from Eaglestone Flat. The cemetery and agricultural features excavated here have been described in the caption for Illustration 9. This particular pot contained the cremation of a woman aged over 50 years and funerary goods including a perforated antler plate and a large flint flake. Environmental analysis of the pyre debris within the pot shows that the cremation had taken place elsewhere and the remains had been brought to this location for burial.

PLATE 7

The Navio Roman fort at Brough in the Hope valley. The first Roman fort was occupied between about AD 75 and AD 120. A somewhat smaller fort, visible in outline in the centre of this aerial shot, was built on the same site in AD 154–8 and remained in use until the mid-fourth century. Excavations have revealed the principal buildings and barracks in the interior, and baths and an extensive civil settlement outside the fort to the east and south (to right and foreground).

PLATE 8

The Benty Grange Helmet; the original (*left*) and how it may once have looked (*right*). This rare find, now in Sheffield City Museum, was manufactured in the late seventh century AD, probably for an important member of the elite of the Pecsaete. It was found

in a typical Anglian barrow high on the ridge top between Monyash and Hartington, associated with a decayed skeleton where only the hair survived, together with chainmail, a leather cup with silver fittings, three escutcheons with silver plate and enamel, and other decayed metal and bone objects.

PLATE 9

The fossilised medieval field system at Tideswell. The present walls and narrow fields fossilise the extensive medieval field pattern here, which covered much of the limestone shelf on which the village is sited. The narrow cultivation strips were enclosed into long and thin walled closes which preserve the general layout of the previously open field. Most strips were enclosed before the Enclosure Award of 1821.

PLATE 10

Tideswell Church. This fine church, known as the Cathedral of the Peak, stands within the largest market centre at the heart of the limestone plateau. The bulk of the present structure was built in the Decorated style in the fourteenth century, with the Perpendicular tower added late in that century.

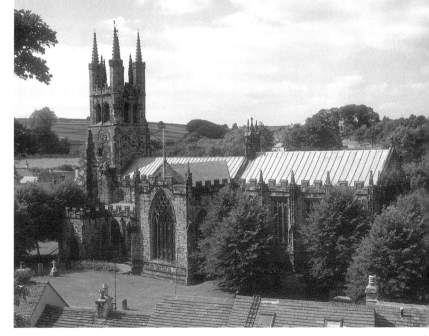

PLATE 11

Peveril Castle above Castleton. This castle, and probably the planned town in the valley below, were built by William Peveril a few years after the Norman Conquest, as a focal point for his extensive Peak District estates granted by William the Conqueror. The eastern bailey was later remodelled in stone. By this time the estates had reverted to the Crown, after William's son poisoned the Earl of Chester in 1155. The keep was built in 1176 over the site of the west gate, as the western bailey was abandoned at this time. The castle as a whole fell out of use after the fourteenth century.

PLATE 12

Chatsworth House from the south-west. The home of the Cavendish family, the earls and later dukes of Devonshire, and one of the grandest stately homes in the country, lies by the Derwent near Edensor, surrounded by gardens and an extensive park. The present house was completed in the early eighteenth century, with the north wing added in the early nineteenth century. The landscape park was created in 1759–60, replacing an earlier deer park on the hillside above, while the present gardens have a long history of development from the late seventeenth century onwards. The building on the skyline was built in the late sixteenth century as hunting tower.

PLATE 13

North Lees Hall, near Hathersage. This fine hall was built in 1591–94, possibly by the architect Smythson. The present domestic wing at the rear was added in the mid-seventeenth century. There are also detached farm outbuildings, including a fine cruck building clad in stone. In the field in front of the house are low terraces marking the site of a small formal garden. The hall was only occupied as such for a short period and soon became a tenanted farmhouse and remained so until restoration in the twentieth century.

PLATE 14

Tideslow Rake, between Tideswell and Little Hucklow. This is a good example of a large lead mining rake which has avoided wholesale modern removal of hillocks, with typical heaps of waste material to either side of the vein, flanking opencasts and run-in shafts to workings deep below.

PLATE 15 (*above*)
The Dane Colliery chimney and Reeve Edge Quarries. This chimney high on moorland was built in the mid-nineteenth century. It was erected at the top end of a flue from a horizontal steam engine adjacent to a coal mine shaft, which operated a continuous rope used to haul coal from the working face to the mine adit entrance. This arched level into the mine is located a short distance further down the valley by the stream, where there is also a ruined mine building. The coal seams here were worked from at least 1746 to 1943. Across the valley are fine examples of old millstone grit quarries with large spoil heaps fed by tramways, the courses of which are still traceable near ruined quarrymen's buildings.

PLATE 16 (*right*)
Derwent Reservoir dam in the Upper Derwent valley. This massive dam, together with that upstream at Howden, was built between 1899 and 1916 by the Derwent Valley Water Board, to provide water for the cities of Sheffield, Derby, Nottingham and Leicester. Nearby are platforms at the site of 'Tin Town' at Birchenlee, a planned settlement for the navvies who worked on this ambitious project.

PLATE 17
Hope Valley Cement Works quarry – an archaeological site of the future? This is one of the largest limestone quarries in the Peak District, lying south-east of Castleton and within the National Park. It illustrates the sometimes conflicting economic and conservation factors that have to be addressed when planning for the future of the region.

A typical continuous feed limekiln near Minninglow. In these more complex continuous feed kilns there was a short tunnel on the downslope side that not only acted as a draught hole, but which could also be used for stoking and to empty the kiln. These kilns could be kept going by feeding fuel and limestone in at the top and taking lime from the bottom, rather than having to empty them after each firing.

types of traditional stile in the region, the squeezer stile with two vertical pillars set close together, and the step stile where three or four long stones were placed horizontally through the wall to provide a stair. While stiles are often found on public footpaths, their presence in a wall does not necessarily denote a right of way, as some were first built by farmers to provide short cuts across their own land, or by miners to gain access to workings.

In many post-medieval fields on the limestone plateau, and occasionally elsewhere, there are small agricultural limekilns. Those on the limestone normally had an adjacent small quarry, although these have often been backfilled in recent years. Field kilns were built to provide lime to improve the quality of grassland and were particularly necessary when land was first taken in from moorland, to burn off rank vegetation and make the soil less acid. This was needed both on the gritstone and the limestone areas, the latter usually having acid soils despite the alkaline bedrock. The most common form is the simple single-chambered circular kiln, called a pie kiln, mostly built in the eighteenth and nineteenth centuries. Limestone and wood or coal were placed in the kiln from the top. After each firing, the lime was dug out, after taking down the downslope side of the kiln. Other forms of intermittent kiln include double and triple clamp kilns, oval in shape with two or three draw holes. These were introduced at the end of the eighteenth century and were thought to be more economic on fuel than single pies. A nineteenth-century kiln type was the relatively large and circular continuous-feed kiln (Figure 45).

Dew ponds are again found commonly on the limestone plateau and sometimes on gritstone uplands. An accessible water supply is rare on the limestone, with only occasional springs. Natural meres, as at Monyash and Heathcote, are even rarer. Once the commons were enclosed and livestock movement restricted, dew ponds were essential for cattle. Sheep, in contrast, do not usually need standing water. Cattle rearing grew in importance in the nineteenth century to supply meat and milk products to nearby cities. Dew ponds collect rainwater, not dew. The method of lining them to make them waterproof, with cobbles, clay, straw and lime, was promoted by a Mr Dew. They were virtually all built in the nineteenth century. Such ponds are disappearing because current farming regulations require mains water for dairy cattle.

CHAPTER EIGHT

Expressions of Power: Church and State in Medieval Times

A place for God: churches and chapels

Domesday Book recorded six pre-Norman churches in the Peak. By the end of the medieval period about 70 churches and chapels existed, reflecting the increasing power of the church at this time. Many villages had their own church in its own ecclesiastical parish. However, the importance of the early churches was often still reflected, even after the Reformation, by their large parishes, which took in several other villages. This was particularly true around Bakewell, where village churches at Baslow, Beeley, Great Longstone, Ashford, Taddington, Monyash and Chelmorton were all technically chapelries within the parish of Bakewell.

A high proportion of the Peak District's medieval churches are still in use today, although a significant number were rebuilt in the Victorian period and little of the original fabric remains. However, there are notable exceptions. Tissington church has a good example of a Norman tower, while Bradbourne church has a fine Norman doorway. Baslow and Hope churches have distinctive thirteenth- and fourteenth-century broach spires. Ashbourne has a graceful church dating from the thirteenth and fourteenth centuries, while at Tideswell there is a particularly impressive example of a fourteenth-century church. Youlgreave church had a massive tower added to the Norman church around the beginning of the fifteenth century. Darley churchyard has a yew tree that may well be over a thousand years old (Colour Plate 10).

A place for the Lord: castles in timber and stone

The Peak District was a political backwater in the medieval period and has relatively few castles. Most are of eleventh- and twelfth-century date and were built of earth and timber. Only their earthworks survive. Early Norman ringworks, comprising circular banks and ditches but no mound for a keep or watchtower, are found next to the church at Hathersage, and possibly at Parwich. More typical mottes and baileys are found at Pilsbury, Bakewell and Bradfield. At Hope and possibly Stony Middleton and Mouselow near Glossop there are damaged mottes where associated earthworks can no longer be traced. At Bank Top, between Pilsbury and Hartington, there is what appears to be an unfinished castle, with a prominent motte but no bailey. Taking these castles together, it is noticeable that the majority are at the manorial centres listed in Domesday Book. The main exception, those in the Dove valley at Pilsbury and Bank Top, are in an area that was waste in 1086, but which soon afterwards became a large manor, eventually dominated by the market centre at nearby Hartington, although the manorial courts continued to be held at the hamlet of Pilsbury until the nineteenth century (Figure 46).

FIGURE 46

Pilsbury Castle as it may have looked in Norman times. Today this castle comprises impressive earthworks on a limestone knoll which dominates the narrow upper Dove valley. The timber castle was probably built in the late eleventh or early twelfth centuries and comprised a motte with bailey and outwork to protect the entrance. It lay at the heart of the De Ferriers estates in the Dove valley and Pilsbury was the administrative centre of the estate; manorial courts were still held in the hamlet into the nineteenth century. However, by the thirteenth century, the village of Hartington, two miles downstream, had become the market centre and was surrounded by extensive open fields.

FIGURE 47
Padley Hall near Hathersage. This modest fourteenth-century hall once had twin courtyards as at Haddon. One range survives to full height, now in use as a chapel, while two other ranges have been reduced to footings, re-exposed in the twentieth century. The sites of two further ranges were destroyed in the nineteenth century when the railway behind the chapel was built. Probable fish ponds survive beyond the railway line.

The one stone castle is Peveril Castle, sited on a high crag above the planned market centre of Castleton in the Hope valley. It probably replaced the early castle at Hope as the manorial centre was transferred a short distance up the valley. Peveril Castle was originally built in timber, with two baileys, its unique situation negating the need for a motte. One bailey, defending the site from the west, still retains its original bank and ditch. The eastern bailey was re-modelled in stone, and a keep added later, when the castle was one of the main administrative centres and gaol for the Royal Forest of the Peak (Colour Plate 11).

A place to live: halls and houses

By far the most impressive medieval hall in the region is that at Haddon, considered in detail in the next chapter. It is an exceptional house and remains of other medieval manorial halls in the region are far less grand. The ruined example at Padley near Hathersage is the most complete. Callow Hall near Wirksworth has a medieval stone undercroft below a later house, the whole surrounded by a moat. Part of what appears to be a gatehouse tower associated with a moat survives at Fenny Bentley. Other post-medieval houses in the region are known to be on the sites of earlier halls and early fabric may await discovery. Moats are rare in the region, with further examples recorded at Ashford, Hartington, Darley, and Snitterton. However, it is not known which are truly medieval defensive works and which are garden features (Figure 47).

Excavations at Roystone Grange, near Ballidon, have shown the monastic grange farmstead here had a late twelfth- or early thirteenth-century aisled timber hall with outer walls of stone. An adjacent small two-storey stone hall was added later in the thirteenth century.

Secular farmhouses in medieval times were generally built of timber as opposed to the stone of church, castle and hall. Typical medieval long houses comprise a rectangular building with dwelling at one end and byre for animals at the other. They are often associated with smaller outbuildings. Platforms for such structures can be seen at deserted and shrunken medieval villages, but none in the region have been excavated to provide detail. Rare stone-footed examples exist at moorland enclosures at Lawrence Field and Sheffield Plantation, both on the gritstone uplands above Hathersage (see Figure 38).

In later medieval times yeoman farmers built substantial cruck-framed halls, a number of which survive in the region, usually disguised within the later stone walls of private houses and barns. A recent series of tree ring dates from their timbers shows they were built in the fifteenth and sixteenth centuries (Figure 48).

A place to hunt: royal forests in the Peak

Large parts of the north-western Peak District were set aside as hunting forests in the medieval period (see Figure 31). These areas were largely uncultivated upland, much never tree covered, surrounded by wooded valleys and farms in clearings. The only villages with open fields lay at the south-eastern fringe.

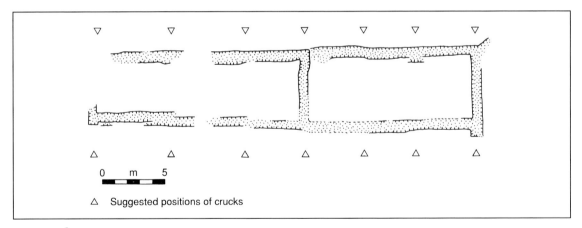

0   m   5

△ Suggested positions of crucks

FIGURE 48
Excavated building at Blackwell Hall Farm, Blackwell. Blackwell township belonged to Lenton Priory from 1108 to 1538 and this building is one of a series of footings recently excavated that may well prove to be part of the demesne farm or grange that acted as the administrative centre for the priory's holdings in the Peak. The excavated buildings appear to have been constructed round a yard and the layout has been modified at least once. The irregular orientation of the excavated walls of the illustrated building is typical of low non-load bearing walls built between the main timbers of cruck buildings. The buildings are therefore probably of late medieval date, and are the hall and outbuildings of the Blackwall family, who farmed Lenton Priory's estate here at that time. By 1631 at the latest all had been demolished, and the farm and outbuildings had been rebuilt on an adjacent site.

These remote areas had only ever been thinly populated and were largely recorded as waste in Domesday Book. The largest part fell within Derbyshire and was the Forest of the Peak, a Royal hunting reserve. Abutting it to the west and running onto the edges of the plain below was Macclesfield Forest in Cheshire, which originally included Leek and Alstonefield Friths in Staffordshire, both once known as Malbanc Frith. These were held in Norman times by the Earls of Chester, who granted the Staffordshire parts to the Malbanc Family. Macclesfield Forest reverted to the Crown in the mid-thirteenth century and became a Royal Forest.

The Royal Forest of the Peak was formally created in the Norman period, although a large part of it had been part of the Royal Manor of Hope in Saxon times and may have been used similarly. In the early twelfth century the north-western part, Longdendale, was added and the forest divided into three districts, Longdendale (North West), Hopedale (North East) and Campana (South). It had its own laws and forest officials and its administration was complex. Peveril Castle was an administrative centre and prison for offenders against forest law. There was a foresters hall at the centre of the forest, at the present village of Peak Forest. The forest courts or eyres were held at Bowden (Chapel en le Frith), Tideswell and Castleton or Hope. Macclesfield Forest had a foresters' chamber high on the moors, close to the present hamlet of Macclesfield Forest. The forest courts were held in Macclesfield where there was also a gaol.

The forest laws were relaxed in the mid-thirteenth century and gradually fell out of use from this time onwards. Significant encroachment into the forests by farmers, some with Crown grants, had started by the mid-thirteenth century. In 1579, in a final attempt to save the Forest of the Peak, a fence was built to contain the last vestige at its heart, around the chamber at Peak Forest. This deer park covered the area defined by the present parish. By the second half of the seventeenth century both Peak Forest and Macclesfield Forest effectively ceased to exist.

Little physical evidence of the medieval forests survives. The main reminders are graves slabs in church porches probably belonging to foresters, including examples carved with axes at Chelmorton, bows and arrows at Bakewell, and swords and horns at Darley and Wirksworth.

At the south-eastern edge of the region, on the infertile sandstone ridges, was another forest, Duffield Frith. This belonged to the Duchy of Lancaster but became Crown land when Henry IV succeeded to the throne in 1399. This heavily wooded area was decimated in the late sixteenth century and surviving parts were finally disafforested in the seventeenth and eighteenth centuries. It also contained a number of fenced parks, some of which continued in use into the post-medieval period although most had lost their deer by this date.

Other private deer parks are poorly documented in the Peak and few seem to have existed. The main exception, and probably the largest, was that at Haddon which is discussed in the next chapter. Others are known to have existed at Harthill, Blore, Okeover and Lyme.

CHAPTER NINE

Building in Stone: Country Houses and Vernacular Buildings

Aristocratic splendour: Chatsworth, Haddon and Lyme

The Peak District contains many halls and manor houses, but three are of particular importance. Two stand less than 5 km (3.1 miles) apart but are in strong contrast to one another. Haddon Hall is one of the best examples in England of a late medieval hall, while Chatsworth House has all the classical splendour of a mansion built after the Renaissance. In this respect, Lyme Hall on the western fringe of the Peak is similar. All three halls and their gardens reflect changing standards of comfort expected by the aristocracy, and an increasing desire to create private spaces for refined living and entertainment, which became increasingly detached from the world outside.

Haddon Hall, south-east of Bakewell, is a large, rectangular crenellated house with two courtyards built by the Vernon family in the late twelfth century. It passed in the mid-sixteenth century to the Manners family, Earls then Dukes of Rutland. Although the present buildings are mostly of fourteenth- and fifteenth-century date, the original house must have been of similar size, as earlier remains occur in all parts except the cross wing. The cross wing contains a grand late medieval great hall and family chambers. Later, part of one of the other ranges was converted to a long gallery overlooking the late sixteenth-century terraced gardens. These originally included a bowling green, moved to a new site in the park in the mid-seventeenth century, when the formal garden was enlarged and remodelled.

The house was little used by the dukes of Rutland in the eighteenth and nineteenth centuries, the main reason it survives in its present form. After this long period of neglect, both house and gardens were restored early in the twentieth century (Figure 49).

The hall and gardens originally stood at the heart of a large medieval deer park. In the seventeenth and eighteenth centuries formal features were added, including two bowling greens and avenues of trees on the hillside above the hall. Little else survives of the park, as it fell out of use in the late eighteenth century and the whole was enclosed and used as farmland. The present much smaller park is a mid-nineteenth-century creation, screened from the road by plantations to create an exclusive private space.

FIGURE 49 (*opposite*) **Haddon Hall from across the River Wye**. This is one of the most splendid examples of a medieval hall in Britain, built on a rocky crag overlooking the River Wye, southeast of Bakewell. In medieval times it stood within a large deer park and there was a village on the other side of the river. The fortified house contains some masonry dating from its foundation in the twelfth century, but the present structure was mostly remodelled 200 to 300 years later. The original gatehouse is upslope to the northeast, while the south-west gate used by visitors today was not added until the early sixteenth century. Outside the hall is a stable block with late medieval fabric and across the late seventeenth-century bridge is a fine early seventeenth-century dovecote (visible in Figure 33).

Chatsworth House, near Edensor, also has medieval origins, although originally probably much less grand than Haddon. The property was transformed when Bess of Hardwick and her husband, Sir William Cavendish, bought the estate in the mid-sixteenth century. A large four-storey courtyard house was built that was of similar size to the present house. In the centuries to the present, there have followed a series of grand building projects, following the latest fashions and displaying the wealth and status of the family. The house was remodelled by the first Duke of Devonshire in the late seventeenth and early eighteenth centuries, using various architects for different phases of the project, including Talman and Sir James Thornhill. In the mid-eighteenth century the stable block was built by James Paine and the large northern wing of the house was added in the early nineteenth century by Sir Jeffrey Wyatville (Colour Plate 12).

The present formal gardens, terraces, impressive lakes and cascades were laid out at the same time as today's house was started. They were altered and added

to over two centuries, with notable additions being made in the nineteenth century by Paxton, including the Emperor Fountain and the now demolished great conservatory which was the inspiration for the Crystal Palace. These private pleasure grounds illustrate changes in perception through time of the way gardens were used to reflect the idealised ways in which the rich perceived their relationship with the world. On the one hand making nature safe, creating an illusion that the house lay within a natural world and thus its existence was beyond question, while on the other flaunting wealth by creating a space that was very different from the outside world.

A walled deer park on the hillside above the house and formal gardens existed in the sixteenth century and fine old oak trees north of the house may date from this phase of the park's history. High above is a late sixteenth-century hunting tower, while between the hall and the mid-eighteenth-century bridge over the Derwent is a moated garden of similar date to the tower, known as Queen Mary's Bower. This, and earthworks nearby, are the last survivals of large formal gardens, ponds and a canal on this side of the house which were removed in the mid-eighteenth century. At this date a large ornamental landscape park spanning both sides of the Derwent was created by Capability Brown, giving the surroundings to the house their present idealised 'natural' appearance, which is of course far from natural. The emparkment left an exceptional earlier agricultural landscape fossilised in low earthwork form, with whole swathes of medieval ridge and furrow and later field boundary banks. Many of the mature oaks and ashes in the Park once stood in hedgerows and were retained to create a ready-made parkland landscape. Later changes included expansions of the park northwards and demolition of part of the village of Edensor in the first half of the nineteenth century. This made it invisible from the house and created an uncluttered and more exclusive approach to the house. What remained was refurbished in an eclectic mixture of decorative architectural styles to create an estate village that was pleasing to the eye and also underlined the power of the Devonshire family and the extent to which locals were dependent on that power and patronage for their jobs and homes (Figure 50).

Lyme Hall, long the home of the Legh family but now managed by the National Trust, is built on a prominent ridge overlooking the park. Like Chatsworth, its architecture is classical surrounding a late sixteenth-century core. There are small ornamental terraced gardens within a large ornamentalised park with impressive avenues of trees, which had earlier origins as a deer park.

From halls to hovels: the Peak District building traditions of the last five centuries

Many of the villages of the Peak have fine halls and manor houses built by the local gentry. Particularly common are late sixteenth- and seventeenth-century houses, stone-built, often with mullioned windows and prominent gables and

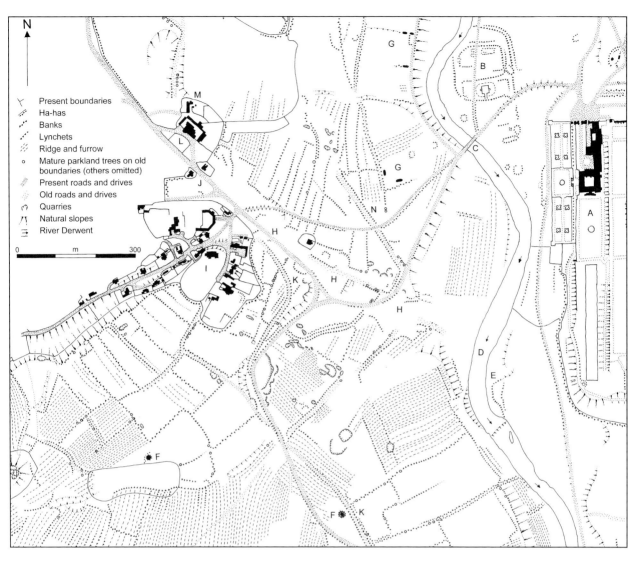

FIGURE 50

Pre-parkland features in the central area of Chatsworth Park. This part of the park, west of Chatsworth House and gardens (A), was mostly created in 1759–60 by Capability Brown. As part of this grand scheme, large formal gardens and ponds near the river were swept away, leaving only Queen Mary's Bower and low earthworks (B). A fine new bridge over the river was built (C), replacing one further downstream (D), near the site of Chatsworth Mill (E). The creation of parkland left faint traces, best seen when under light snow, of the previous use of the land. Most of the eighteenth-century field boundaries around Edensor survive as slight banks, often with ridge and furrow within the fields, much of which has medieval origins. Pronounced strip lynchets are the most obvious traces of the medieval strip fields. Amongst the fields there are surviving prehistoric barrows (F). In the centuries immediately before the park was created the area north-east of the village was a warren where rabbits were reared and artificial mounds were built for the rabbits to live in (G). Many of the maturest trees standing today in this part of the park lie on the redundant field boundaries, which suggests they were growing by the mid-eighteenth century, rather than planted at the time the park was created. Various modifications were made to the parkland landscape after it was first created. The most radical was the remodelling of Edensor in the 1820s–40s, with the levelling of the village's eastern half (H) and remodelling of the buildings in the western half in a variety of architectural styles to create a picturesque model village (I). This allowed an unobstructed route into the park, with new lodges (J) and drives built. An earlier drive is clearly visible running south (K). The present Estate Oyce (L) started life as a coaching inn and an eighteenth-century lodge behind (M) was part of an aborted scheme to build a drive (N) behind the old village.

chimneys. These houses represent a flourish of building using stone, often for the first time, outwardly displaying status and permanency, linked with increased wealth in the region derived from lead mining. Typical examples include halls at Snitterton, Eyam, Highlow near Hathersage, and Hartington. Others at North Lees near Hathersage, Tissington and Holme near Bakewell were designed with elements of Jacobean style found at grander houses elsewhere in surrounding regions. Stone halls were rare prior to the seventeenth century, with the exception of medieval examples noted in Chapter 8. One further exception is the hall at Hazlebadge near Bradwell, now a roadside farmhouse where the surviving wing dates to the mid-sixteenth century. The modest late seventeenth-century hall at Castleton is built with a classical front and heralds the architecture of the next century (Colour Plate 13).

Relatively few halls have been built in the region in the last 300 years. Modest halls in the classical style typical of the eighteenth century were built in stone at Winster, Stoke Hall near Grindleford, and Ashford, and in brick at Great Longstone and Parwich. The classical tradition continued into the nineteenth century with the rebuilding of Hassop Hall, one of the largest residences to be built in the region, surpassed only by Chatsworth and Lyme. The nineteenth century also saw the building of halls in gothic style at Middleton by Youlgreave, and in eclectic Jacobean style at Thornbridge Hall and Churchdale Hall, both near Ashford (Figure 51).

The traditional vernacular architecture of the region is characterised by buildings in local stone, both limestone and gritstone. Of the two, gritstone was more suitable for shaping and was imported onto the limestone plateau for details such as door and window surrounds. Walls are usually of irregularly laid stones, sometimes roughly coursed. The use of gritstone ashlar was only occasionally employed, mainly from the late nineteenth century onwards. Thinly bedded local sandstones provided roofing flags. Once the norm, they can still be seen occasionally but are increasingly being replaced due to their unavailability, as they are no longer quarried.

The farmhouses and cottages seen today usually date from the seventeenth century onwards, although a few hide late-medieval crucks within later stone-cladding. Occasionally chamfered-mullion windows can be seen, showing buildings to be of seventeenth-century date. More common are eighteenth- and nineteenth-century buildings. Farmhouses are commonly an integral part of a single building-range which incorporates the outbuildings at one end, including byre and hay-barn. This layout is found at small farmsteads built from at least the seventeenth century onwards and may well have medieval origins. Larger farmsteads have more than one range of buildings, usually accreted over time. There is a variety of plans, with ranges often built parallel or at right angles. Only occasionally did these develop into closed courtyards. Buildings of two storeys are the norm, although three-storey farmhouses of eighteenth- and nineteenth-century date can occasionally be seen. Only minor outbuildings such as pigsties and cart sheds are of one storey. It was once the norm for cottages also to have accompanying pigsties, stables or cow sheds, and cart sheds; where they survive these have now been converted to other uses.

One characteristic of much of the region is the number of barns, together with occasional smaller byres and sheds, found scattered in fields away from villages and farms. The field barns are typically eighteenth- and nineteenth-century buildings of two storeys, with cattle stalling below and hay storage above. Smaller one-storey examples are also common. The presence of field barns reflects the division of land into parcels sited well away from dwellings, either on land enclosed from common or waste, or in enclosed open fields. Farmers found it convenient to provide shelter and food for livestock within these land parcels, rather than transport stock or hay. In some cases the barn was essential, as the farmers were smallholders whose main employment was in other trades such as lead mining or carting, and their dwellings had no suitable adjacent outbuildings. Unfortunately, most field barns are now incompatible with modern farming practices and have been neglected. Many

FIGURE 51 (*opposite*)
Hassop Hall from within the park. This hall, now a hotel, is a fine example of an early nineteenth-century house surrounded by a park of similar date. Both house and park have much earlier origins, but were remodelled by the Earl of Newburgh. The house was enlarged and classicized in 1827–33. Some outbuildings, including an orangery and a ballroom linked to the hall by an underground passage, were built at the same time, while others date from the 1850s.

have been demolished or lie derelict, although a few have been saved by conversion to camping barns (Figure 52).

The nineteenth century saw a flurry of building at parish churches, including the restoration of many medieval churches. There was radical rebuilding at important examples, such as Bakewell and Wirksworth. Several new parish churches were also built, in a variety of styles. These include classical examples at Hassop and Buxton, and gothic ones at Edensor and Edale. Most of the region's non-conformist chapels were also built in the nineteenth century, ranging from severely plain early examples, such as that at Barber Booth, in Edale, to gothic examples, such as that at Middleton by Youlgreave, built later in the century (Figure 53).

FIGURE 52

Field barns on the limestone plateau above Bakewell. Field barns are common in the region. Traditionally many farms and smallholdings had parcels of fields located at a distance from the farmstead or house. These often had a barn where cattle could be stalled, with hay stored above. They are particularly common around market centres like Bakewell and where lead mining was very extensive as at Winster and Bonsall, all areas where people commonly had dual incomes.

FIGURE 53
The village of Edensor within Chatsworth Park. With the exception of one house, that part of the village of Edensor nearest Chatsworth House was demolished by the sixth Duke of Devonshire in 1838–42 to give an uncluttered approach to the house. The far part of the village was remodelled in the 1820s–40s, with new frontages and some new dwellings, as a 'picturesque' model village designed by Paxton and Robertson. The church, by Sir George Gilbert Scott, was added in 1867.

Two settlements in the Peak District stand out from all others. Both Buxton and Matlock grew dramatically in size in the eighteenth and nineteenth centuries, developed as fashionable spa resorts. Buxton was promoted by the dukes of Devonshire who owned much of the land. Of its fashionable buildings, including shops, hotels and residences, pre-eminent is The Crescent. The massive stable block behind was later converted into the Devonshire Hospital and is now being developed as a university campus. The town also boasts a fine nineteenth-century pavilion and theatre complex, the former an impressive steel-framed and glass-domed structure. Matlock is dominated by a huge mid-nineteenth-century hydro, now the County Council offices, while Matlock Bath nearby has houses and shops built to serve the tourist trade and a rather ugly pavilion now housing the Peak District Mining Museum.

Other settlements grew in post-medieval times due to their proximity to rich lead-mines. This is most noticeable at Bradwell and Winster, where the villages expanded up steep hills towards the mines (Figure 54).

FIGURE 54

Winster from the air. This village, at the edge of the limestone plateau, has a small medieval core at the base of the hill. With the increase of lead-mining on the limestone plateau above, reaching its height in the seventeenth and eighteenth centuries, houses were rebuilt, some with pretensions of grandeur. The settlement grew, with expansion taking place uphill, to the right, to cut down the walking distance to the mines.

CHAPTER TEN

Packhorses and Turnpikes: Roads Through the Ages

Braided ways and paved paths: traditional routes through the Peak

Before the building of modern roads, starting in the eighteenth century with turnpikes, the roads of the region were mostly rough tracks. Around villages, running through enclosed farmland, were walled lanes. Sometimes these became deeply hollowed where rising up steep slopes, particularly when underlain by sandstones and shales which are more susceptible to erosion than limestone. Once the routeways reached the open commons and wastes people were free to roam at will and they often spread out to avoid previous tracks that had become boggy. After many years, the end result was braided hollow-ways, with sunken tracks from a few centimetres to a couple of metres deep, criss-crossing each other in swathes, sometimes over a hundred metres wide. The antiquity of these tracks is demonstrated where they are overlain by road-side and field walls of farmland enclosed from common 150 to 250 years ago. The braided ways mostly take relatively direct routes where there are no major topographic obstacles. Boggy ground may well have only been passable in dry weather. More circuitous winter routes can sometimes be traced.

There is also a number of paved causeways, usually comprising a single continuous line of slabs. Paved paths are being built today on Kinder as a method of erosion control. Unlike the modern examples, the old paved paths are mostly grown over and difficult to find. An exception to this exists above Stanage Edge, where an eighteenth-century paved cartway running past Stanage Pole has often been confused with a Roman road. This is joined by a single line of recently cleared and renovated slabs, which runs down the Edge, through Stanage Plantation, to the car park below (Figures 55, 56).

Where routeways met streams and rivers they were either forded or bridged. The latter varied from simple clappers over narrow streams, to fine bridges. Early bridges wide enough for cart traffic survive, for example, at Bakewell and Baslow. There are also several classic packhorse bridges, often of seventeenth-century date, just wide enough for a single string of horses. Well known in-situ examples are those in Edale at the foot of Jacob's Ladder, at Grindsbrook and at Holme near Bakewell. Those high in the Derwent and Goyt valleys were moved when their original sites were flooded beneath reservoirs.

FIGURE 55

A hollow way at Lawrence Field, near Hathersage. This route, which came from Hathersage, here ran down a deep hollow way, crossed the stream and spread out with many braids on the broad shelf beyond, heading towards Chesterfield. This route was already disused when the Duke of Rutland built his shooting lodge at Longshaw, hidden in the trees in the background.

While many of the individual hollows in braided hollow-ways are narrow, indicating use by foot and packhorse traffic, wider tracks suitable for carts and wagons can also be identified. In places deep trench-ways are cut to bedrock, with much rubble cleared from them and placed to the side. It was a statutory parish duty to maintain highways from the mid-sixteenth century onwards.

Spaced along many of the main routes are guidestones, used as waymarkers at skyline locations and at junctions. These are often pillar-like, with colloquially spelt destinations inscribed on their faces. Sometimes there are

FIGURE 56 (*opposite*)

Hollow ways and turnpikes on Big Moor, north-east of Baslow. This part of the eastern gritstone moors provides a good example of surviving earthworks of pre-turnpike routes. These can be seen as braided hollow ways, with occasional guide stones and crosses. They fell out of use when the turnpike roads were built between the mid-eighteenth and early nineteenth centuries. Although the new roads often took slightly different routes, they were constrained by the same natural obstacles as before.

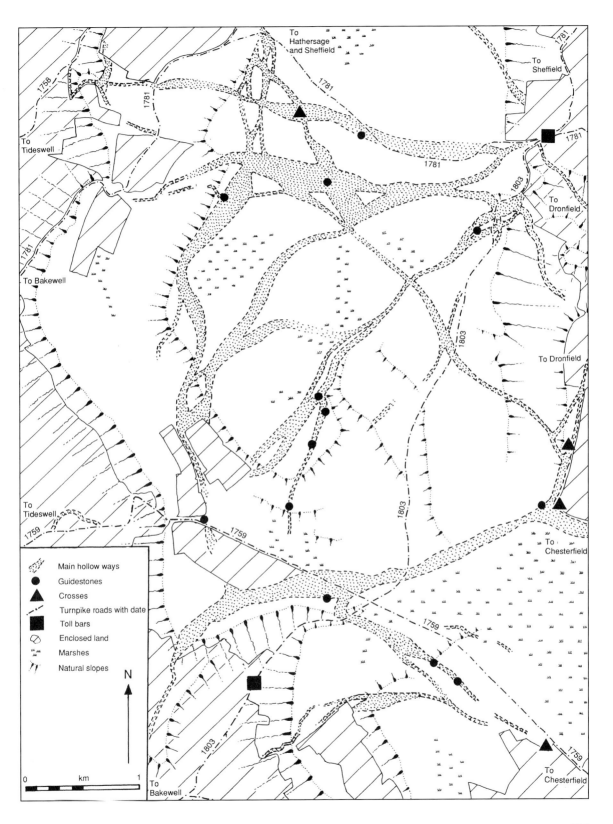

To Hathersage
and Sheffield

To Sheffield

To Tideswell

To Dronfield

To Bakewell

To Dronfield

To Tideswell

To Chesterfield

Main hollow ways
Guidestones
Crosses
Turnpike roads with date
Toll bars
Enclosed land
Marshes
Natural slopes

N

0   km   1

To Bakewell

To Chesterfield

also the carved initials of the Road Commissioners who inspected them in the eighteenth century. Good examples can be seen on Big Moor and east of Hob Hurst's House on Harland Edge above Beeley (Figure 57).

Braided hollow-ways are common on the gritstone moorlands, particularly running east and west, the main directions of flow for trade across the region. Traditional exports included lead, millstones and agricultural produce such as wool. Items brought in or through the region included salt from Cheshire, and many products from the industrial centres either side of the Pennines. Saltways can be reconstructed from placename evidence.

Not all hollow ways were communication or trade routes. Some ran from settlements to pastures, watering places, local stone quarries and peat cuts. In contrast, tracks for millstones can be traced on the eastern moors running from the quarries eastwards for long distances, heading ultimately to the port of Bawtry. Grooves made by millstones, which were rolled on edge in pairs

FIGURE 57
A guidestone at Edensor, near Bakewell. The two visible faces, each with a hand indicating direction, say 'Chesterfield Rode' and 'Sheyeld Rode'. A third face indicates 'Bakewell Rode', with the date 1709. The use of lower case letters is unusual in the Peak District at this time. The fourth face is blank.

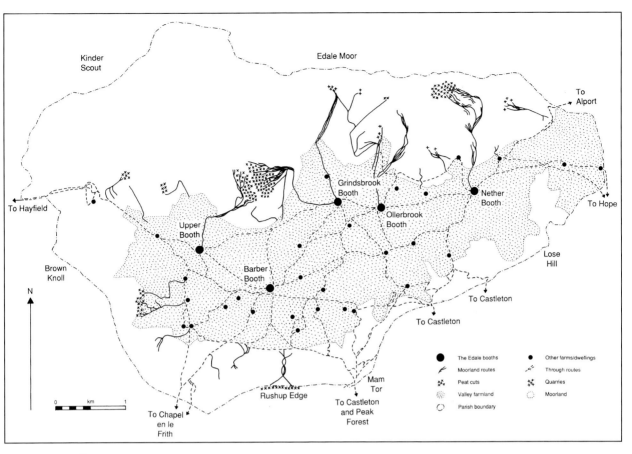

FIGURE 58
Hollow ways and sled routes in the Edale valley. A large number of abandoned routes run up the steep sides of the Edale Valley on to the high moorlands above. In addition to communication routes, there are sled ways and cart roads to peat cuts and quarries. The distribution of these suggests that each of the five Booths in the valley used specific moors where they had traditional rights of peat cutting (turbary) that may well go back to medieval times. Peat cutting ceased here in the nineteenth century when cheap coal became available.

with a short axle between, have recently been identified where they sank into peaty soils (Figure 58).

Laying a firm way: building the modern road network

Turnpike roads were carefully made toll roads which transformed communication and transportation in the eighteenth century. The roads had hardcore foundations, with cobbled or, later, asphalt surfaces, and could stand heavy traffic in all weathers. They had drainage ditches to either side where necessary and ran on causeways across wet ground. Often they were walled to prevent illicit traffic entering or leaving them between toll gates.

The earliest routes in the Peak to be turnpiked were the Derby to Manchester road, different sections of which were improved between 1724 and 1749, and the Chesterfield to Bakewell road which was turnpiked in 1739. During the second half of the eighteenth century and the early nineteenth cen-

FIGURE 59

Turnpike milestones in the Peak District. Each turnpike trust had its own design of milestone or milepost, some of which are illustrated here. This gritstone milepost is on the Totley to Stoney Middleton turnpike of 1781 (now the B6054). It indicates the distances to Gleadless (Sheffield) and Calver.

This cast-iron milepost is on the Chesterfield to Baslow turnpike of 1812 (now the A619), 6 miles from Chesterfield. Out of view, it indicates the miles to Baslow – 2; Bakewell – 6; Buxton – 17; and Manchester – 38. In a typical grandiose gesture it also shows the distance to London.

This milepost, in cast iron on a gritstone upright, is on the Greenfield and Shepley Lane Head turnpike of 1823/24, across Wessenden Moor (now the A635).

This carved gritstone milestone is north of the village of Holme, on the Holme to Woodhead turnpike, also of 1823/24 (now the A6024).

FIGURE 60
The tollhouse at Ringinglow. This impressive tollhouse is positioned at the junction of turnpike roads built in 1758 running from Sheffield to Buxton and to Chapel en le Frith (and ultimately on to Manchester).

tury much of the present road network was laid out. Tolls were paid until the late nineteenth century when the responsibility for road upkeep passed to local authorities.

The late eighteenth and early nineteenth centuries saw the diversion of stretches of many of the earlier turnpikes. Originally these had often taken relatively direct routes and included excessively steep gradients. These new bypasses took longer, more circuitous routes to overcome this problem. Occasionally new routes altogether were adopted.

Abandoned stretches of eighteenth-century turnpikes still exist as green lanes. Good examples are the track from Fox House above Hathersage to Ringinglow on the outskirts of Sheffield, the track from Burbage to Derbyshire Bridge in the upper Goyt Valley, and those to either side of the Longhill road from Buxton to Whaley Bridge. Occasionally totally abandoned stretches of turnpike road are found running over moor and through fields, their causeways often still with their original cobbled surfaces beneath a thin turf.

Other vestiges of the turnpike era survive. By the side of the roads are milestones in stone or cast iron, dating from the late eighteenth and early nineteenth centuries. Each turnpike trust is identifiable by its uniquely designed stones. There are also toll houses. These are often only recognisable from their names, but occasionally they have distinctive architecture, as with the large octagonal example at Ringinglow (Figures 59, 60).

CHAPTER ELEVEN

Mines, Mills and Quarries: Industrial Monuments from Medieval Times Onwards

....

Industrial wastelands or places of beauty

Few visitors admiring the beauty of the Peak District realise that traditionally it has been important for its industry. From medieval times to the twentieth century, much of the landscape has been scarred by quarrying, by bare waste heaps from lead- and coal-mines and by limekilns and quarries. Lead-mine waste heaps poisoned the ground, while the smelting works also poisoned the air. Running between the mines, mills and quarries and the industrial cities flanking the region there were extensively eroded packhorse routes. With time, old scars have healed and the relics of the various industries add greatly to the interest of the landscape (Figure 61).

Wealth from the rocks: mining for lead and coal

Although the Romans are known to have mined lead in the region (see Chapter 4), the first surviving documentation of this important industry and its customs dates to several hundred years later. Lead extraction was already extensive in late Anglo-Saxon times. This is illustrated by the annual rent of 300 shillings' worth of lead which was paid in the ninth century to Christ Church, Canterbury by the abbey at Repton, which controlled the mines in the manor of Wirksworth. Prior to that, a lead coffin had been made in AD 714 for St. Guthlau, Abbess of Repton. Domesday Book of 1086 records taxable lead works, probably smelters rather than mines, at each of the extensive royal manors of Matlock, Wirksworth, Ashford and Bakewell. Part of Hope manor's annual tax was five wagon loads, each of 50 lead sheets. These entries show that the entire orefield, which covers much of the limestone plateau though most of the larger veins are in its eastern half, was being exploited by the time of the Norman Conquest.

    The medieval lead-miners had their own complex set of customs concerning rights of search, how mines should be worked, and payment in lead or money to the owners of the mineral rights and to the Church. These customs

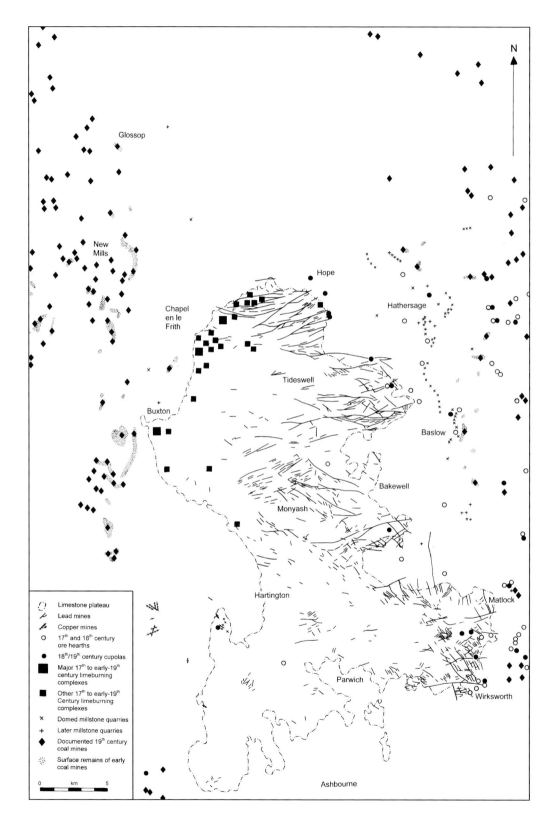

N

Glossop

New
Mills

Chapel
en le
Frith

Hope

Hathersage

Buxton

Tideswell

Baslow

Bakewell

Monyash

Hartington

Matlock

Limestone plateau
Lead mines
Copper mines
17th and 18th century
ore hearths
18th/19th century cupolas
Major 17th to early-19th
century limeburning
complexes
Other 17th to early-19th
Century limeburning
complexes
Domed millstone quarries
Later millstone quarries
Documented 19th century
coal mines
Surface remains of early
coal mines

Parwich

Wirksworth

0   km   5

Ashbourne

were formalised into a set of laws in the late thirteenth century which formed
the basis for lead extraction to the present century. The laws were enforced in
Barmoot Courts, by the main officials, the Barmaster and Steward. The
orefield was divided into areas called Liberties, each with minor variations in
law and custom.

There is a tradition in the Peak District of small-scale mining undertaken
by miner/farmers, who practised both occupations, mining at slack times of
the agricultural year. This tradition has a long history, over many centuries.
Local mining law divided veins into short sections called Meers, between 28
and 32 yards (26 and 29m) long, which had to be kept in work or they could
be claimed by other miners. These divisions favoured small-scale mining. Only
with the advent of deep mining below the water-table, from the seventeenth
century onwards, was there an increased need for capital investment in larger
mining ventures. This change is consistent with the transformation of many
industries as part of the developing ideological change from a feudal to a
capitalist society. Even so, in the nineteenth century, while larger mines
employed full time miners often working deep underground, smaller veins
were still being worked near the surface in traditional fashion.

The bulk of the lead in the orefield is found in veins. The larger ones, often
1–2 metres (3–6ft) wide, are known as Rakes, while minor veins, often only a
few centimetres across, are called Scrins. Occasionally further ore was found
in flat works running horizontally with the strata, or in 'pipes' which were very
variable in size and were locally rich, the mineralisation here deposited in
ancient cave or cave-like passages. Rakes often run for miles across the limestone plateau, with a roughly east/west trend, mostly cutting near-vertically
into the ground. Lead ore, usually galena, was only one of several minerals
within a typical vein. Copper and zinc were occasionally present, but non-met-
alliferous minerals of calcite, fluorspar and barytes normally made up more
than 90 per cent of any vein. These were of little value and were left on surface site in extensive waste heaps, or stacked underground in redundant
workings. However, their usefulness to modern industry has led to widespread
removal of the heaps and the reworking of veins over the last 100 years, resulting in extensive destruction of important archaeological remains of the earlier
lead mining industry (Colour Plate 14).

The earliest mining was probably mostly opencast along rakes, followed
later by shallow shafts to underground workings or stopes along the veins. Ore
was extracted by picks and by hammer and wedges. Where limestone also
needed to be removed, in order to follow thin mineralised veins or flats, the
laborious technique of fire-setting had to be used to fracture the rock. Recent

FIGURE 61 (*opposite*)
Map showing the main traditional industrial resources of the Peak District. Resources cluster in specific regions. The
limestone plateau was the main source of metaliferous wealth and was used for lime production, while in contrast the
areas beyond were a source of coal and of millstones and pulpstones. Smelting sites concentrated to the east between the
sources of lead and of coal and timber.

research underground has identified evidence for firesetting using coal at several accessible mines, of probable medieval or early post-medieval date, where there is also extensive sooting from the smoke. Exceptional mines occur at the Nestus Pipes at Matlock Bath, that have had rich pipe mineralisation removed with small picks. Over 670m (615ft) of passages are accessible, making them one of the largest medieval mines in Britain and parts of these workings are readily visible in the Great Masson Cavern and Rutland Cavern show caves. It was not until the second half of the seventeenth century that gunpowder was introduced. This allowed extraction rates to be significantly increased and enabled the driving of long levels and deep shafts in solid limestone.

By the seventeenth century most of the main rakes had been worked down to the water table, typically 50 to 100m (150 to 300ft) below the surface. The need to dig deeper at this time led to the installation of water wheels for pumping and the driving of the first drainage levels, known locally as soughs. These are a particular feature of the orefield and something like 500 are documented. Early examples of these were often driven only short distances into hillsides, sometimes from stream or river level, to lower the local water table. One of the first was Vermuyden's Sough to the Gang Mines near Middleton by Wirksworth, started in 1631. An ambitious sough at Cromford, the modified tail of which is still visible in the village, was begun in about 1657–58 and continued to be driven intermittently for well over 100 years by which time it was well over 2km (1.5 miles) long. The eighteenth century saw still more ambitious soughs being driven, such as Stoke Sough and Magclough Sough, both driven from the River Derwent to de-water the mines under Eyam Edge. The last major sough was driven between 1873 and 1881, from the River Wye to Magpie Mine near Sheldon.

The eighteenth century also saw the introduction of steam-powered pumps of Newcomen-type for lifting water from lower workings, by which time the use of horses for winding ores out of deeper shafts had become common. Such shafts usually had a large horizontal drum for the winding ropes erected adjacent to the shaft head, known as a horse gin. In the nineteenth century a few of the largest mines introduced steam winding engines, at first of Cornish-type beam-arm type, while later horizontal engines were used. Large Cornish pumping engines were also built, as at Magpie Mine. The deepest of these engine shafts, at over 330m (1082ft), was at New Engine Mine above Eyam Edge.

Large speculative mining ventures occurred in the eighteenth and first half of the nineteenth centuries. Massive amounts of capital were sunk into mines at Eyam and Alport where major veins had been located in limestone overlain by shale and gritstone beds, first found early in the eighteenth century and still not worked out a hundred years later. Other examples of large mining ventures were Odin Mine at Castleton, High Rake west of Great Hucklow, Mandale Mine at Over Haddon and Magpie Mine near Sheldon, all worth visiting today because of the surviving surface features (Figure 62).

FIGURE 62
Magpie Mine, near Sheldon. This mine already existed before the nineteenth century, at which date there were several attempts to mine at depth using then state of the art technology. The Cornish engine house which dominates the scene was built in 1869 adjacent to a large shaft, which eventually reached 220m (722ft) deep. This was used for pumping water from the mine to enable ore extraction below the water table. There are several other nineteenth-century buildings surviving on site, built at various dates from the first half of the nineteenth century onwards, including a winding house, boiler house and chimneys, a miners' dry, an ore house, a small dressing floor engine house, an agent's house and smithy, and the isolated powder house. Taken together, they represent one of the best surviving nineteenth-century mine complexes in Britain. The mine closed in 1883 but was again worked intermittently on a smaller scale in the twentieth century and the headgear above the shaft dates from the 1950s. Nearby there are several other grilled shafts and the sites of horse gins and dressing floors.

In the second half of the nineteenth century the lead-mining industry went into rapid decline as the major capital ventures failed. In 1861 there were over 2000 men employed in the industry. By 1901 this had fallen to under 300. The only notable exception to the downward trend was the exceptionally rich Millclose Mine at Darley Dale, which didn't close until 1939.

Today, the still-extant surface remains of the lead-mining industry comprise waste hillocks in distinctive lines across the landscape. Amongst the hillocks, which should only be explored with great care, are hollows along the veins, occasionally opening into stopes many metres deep. Also common are shafts, run-in, capped or still open. They vary from climbing shafts less than a metre across, to large winding shafts over 3m (10ft) wide. At later mines, the sites of horse gins can be found, comprising flat, circular areas adjacent to shafts. A handful of engine houses also survive. Other features found occasionally include crushing circles, a variety of ruined mine buildings, ore processing and water storage ponds and stone-lined hollows known as buddles, where crushed material was mixed with water and the heavy lead ore separated from other lighter minerals.

Mines should not be entered. Adits and stopes often have shafts in their floors, while the main hazard is the danger of roof-falls. Normal mining practice was to stack waste rock above the miners' heads in worked-out stopes, often supported on timbers which are now rotten. On the surface, open shafts are equally dangerous as their upper parts are supported by drystone walling or ginging, which is now potentially unstable. However, all this said, several mines can be visited in safety. The Peak District Mining Museum at Matlock Bath opens Temple Mine nearby, and all the currently open show 'caves' in Matlock Bath are pipe workings. The Speedwell Mine at Castleton is unusual in that the mine access tunnel was designed as an underground canal and tourists enter it by boat.

Medieval lead smelting was in boles, which were simple open-air hearths, where the ores were burnt using timber and the slags re-smelted using coal. Boles relied on strong natural draughts and were placed on hilltops, mostly to the east of the limestone plateau. They can be recognised from placenames such as Bolehill, but there is usually little surface evidence, except for contaminated soil and traces of slag. In the mid-sixteenth century there was a radical change in smelting technology with the introduction of smelting mills with water-powered bellows to raise smelting temperature. These mills were sited on small streams feeding the Derwent and in the foothills east of the eastern gritstone moors. These areas had the advantage of large valley-side woodlands. The smelting process often used dried wood, known as white coal. Kilns for drying the white coal survive in several woods, sometimes retained by drystone walling at the inner edge. They look superficially like small, prehistoric, circular house-footings. In the eighteenth century smelting technology again changed with the introduction of reverbatory furnaces, known locally as cupolas. These used coal for firing and had no need to be located near water, and many were placed near coal sources. They were sometimes sited in relatively remote areas because of the highly toxic fumes they emitted. However, there was a number sited relatively close to Sheffield and Chesterfield, placed to the west and upwind of these population centres. Smelters of all periods lay predominantly to the east side of the orefield, as the smelted lead was mostly taken from here to the port of Hull, from where it was exported widely.

Two other mining industries on the limestone plateau are worthy of note. At Ecton Hill, near Warslow in Staffordshire, there were exceptionally rich copper mines which were worked from the early seventeenth to the late nineteenth century. The peak in production was in the second half of the eighteenth century, when for nearly thirty years it was one of the richest copper mines in Britain. Surface remains include a 1780s Boulton and Watt engine house, ruined nineteenth-century mine buildings, adit entrances, gin circles, shafts, and impressive pipe entrances and hillocks. Some of the smaller hillocks and hollows may well be prehistoric in origin (see Chapter 4). Underground, behind locked gates, there are long drainage adits, impressive engine chambers, large pipe workings, and below river level flooded workings that are over 300m deep. At Castleton, a decorative variety of fluorspar, known as Blue John, has been worked from the eighteenth century for ornaments and jewellery. Two mines, Blue John Cavern and Treak Cliff Cavern, are open to the public.

The moorlands at the eastern and western fringes of the Peak District still retain surface evidence of coal mining. The seams that outcropped on these high gritstone uplands were often relatively thin compared with those exploited in the adjacent lowlands beyond the region. Some mines were started in medieval times and many were at work in the eighteenth and early nineteenth centuries. Most went into decline later in that century because of the thinness of the coal seams, the remote locations and economically unviable prospects when expensive drainage schemes would have been necessary to follow the seams at depth, below the local water-table.

The earliest Peak District coal mines were small opencast pits at outcrops, while shafts were sunk to reach the coal seams at greater depth. Closely-spaced shafts continued in use until the first half of the nineteenth century. Deeper examples with horse gins to draw up coal date from the eighteenth century onwards. In the late eighteenth century the particularly important Goyt's Moss and Axe Edge mines, west of Buxton, brought coal to the surface via an underground canal. In the nineteenth century deeper reserves were exploited at a few collieries from adits and engine shafts, with extensive pillar and stall workings underground. These had only occasional shafts to the surface, used for access and ventilation. Such shafts usually have large spoil heaps, while the adits are now often ephemeral. Traces of associated buildings sometimes survive.

The mines to the west centred on valleys from Whaley Bridge northwards, extending virtually to Oldham. There were southern outliers high on the moors, around the head of the Goyt and Dane rivers south-west of Buxton, and at Goldsitch Moss south-west of Flash (Figure 63; Colour Plate 15).

To the east, most mines were located in the foothills west of Chesterfield, Sheffield and Barnsley. At the western edge of this extensive coalfield there are surviving remains which occur intermittently on the higher uplands, as for example above Stanage Edge north-east of Hathersage, and around Robin Hood east of Baslow.

The surface remains commonly comprise closely spaced run-in shafts, each surrounded by waste heaps, sometimes with gin circles and accessed by causeways across wet ground. While such evidence survives in the Peak, in the adjacent lowlands at the heart of the coalfields, they have usually been swept

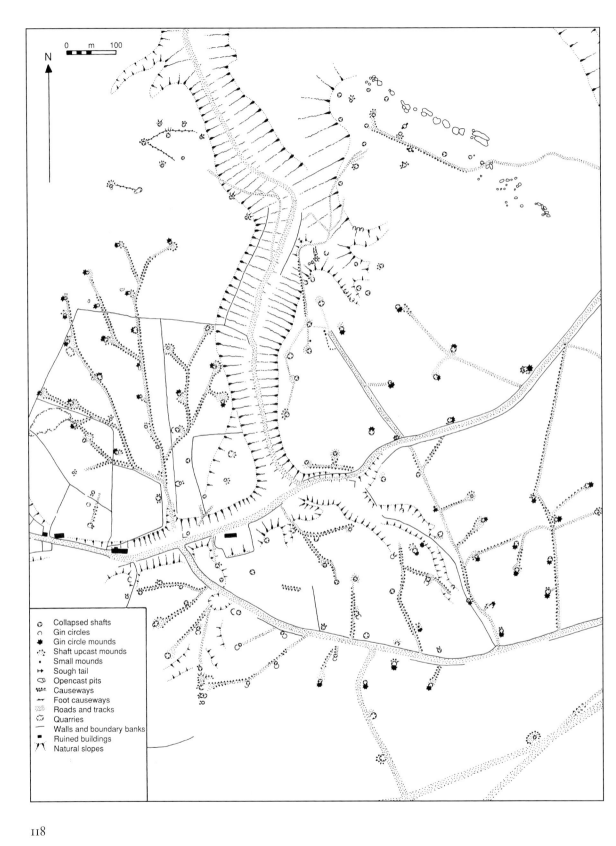

0   m   100

N

Collapsed shafts
Gin circles
Gin circle mounds
Shaft upcast mounds
Small mounds
Sough tail
Opencast pits
Causeways
Foot causeways
Roads and tracks
Quarries
Walls and boundary banks
Ruined buildings
Natural slopes

away by later development, which makes the Peak sites of particular importance.

Wealth from the soil: peat cutting and woodland industries

The soils of the region were not only used for agriculture but were themselves a valuable resource in the form of peat for fuel. They also provided the medium for growing trees for several industrial processes.

Medieval documentation of rights of turbary, the cutting of peat or turf on common land, for villages on the limestone plateau illustrates that many higher areas of the wastes and commons here, enclosed in post-medieval times and now improved farmland, may well once have had deposits of peat or peaty soils. Large peat cuts can still be identified in the Dark Peak high above both the Edale and Upper Derwent valleys, used by local farming communities for fuel since medieval times to the nineteenth century. Smaller peat cuts, used by individual farms and cottages, are known on the western gritstone moorlands.

Many of the ancient woodlands in the Peak District are thought to have been felled in the seventeenth and eighteenth centuries to meet the growing need for timber props for the lead mining industry. However, to either side of the eastern gritstone upland there are woods with indirect evidence for coppice management in the sixteenth to eighteenth centuries. Here wood was dried to produce white coal for use in ore smelting hearths. Also, a large number of charcoal burners' platforms have been identified in the upper Derwent valley. These were extensively used in the eighteenth century to provide charcoal for the iron smelting industry in the Yorkshire foothills around Sheffield. Some have earlier origins, predating the early seventeenth century and may well have been used for local lead smelting, as illustrated by the recent excavation of a small medieval smelting site at Linch Clough.

The power of water: the use of rivers and streams for mills

Water mills have existed in the region since at least late Saxon times. Domesday Book (1086) records mills at Bakewell, Ashford and Youlgreave. Several further examples are recorded in subsequent medieval sources. All these structures were probably small, primarily serving local demand for flour production. The first industrial mills, other than the small lead ore hearths noted above, were built for textiles in the late eighteenth century. The majority were

FIGURE 63 (*opposite*)
Coal mines in the Upper Goyt Valley, west of Buxton. These mines, at over 400m (1312ft) above sea level, comprise a series of run-in shafts with upcast mounds, once about 20–25m (66–82ft) deep, linked by causeways crossing the peat-covered moor. They were part of what became the nineteenth-century Goyt Moss Colliery. The earliest working of the seam near the surface probably took place in the seventeenth century, and the deeper shafts with causeways were dug in the eighteenth and early nineteenth centuries. Later this century mining at depth extended to the south and east, reached by long adits from the east, nearer to Buxton. The mine closed in the 1880s.

large cotton-mills, although a number of wool-, flax- and silk-mills also operated in the region.

The River Derwent and its tributaries supported a series of important late eighteenth-century cotton mills. Several were built by Arkwright, using his water-frame roller-spinning machines, and were some of the earliest mechanised mills. His first mill was built in Cromford in 1771, followed by mills at Cressbrook, Ashbourne, Bakewell, Wirksworth, and Matlock Bath. Other important contemporary mills were built by competitors at Litton, Calver,

FIGURE 64

Cressbrook Mill. This impressive mill, on the River Wye between Litton and Little Longstone, was built in 1815 by William Newton and replaced Arkwright's mill of 1783. The classical exterior masks large open-plan floors supported on cast-iron columns. The clock and bell cupola were added in 1837 to celebrate Queen Victoria's accession to the throne. Most of the ruined buildings in the foreground have now been demolished and the rest of the building remains derelict.

Bamford and Edale. By the beginning of the nineteenth century the focus was beginning to move to the north-west, centred on the rivers Goyt and Etherow. Although still in Derbyshire, this area lay within the Lancashire cotton production area. By this time, there were as many mills in this part of Derbyshire as the rest of the county put together. Through the rest of the nineteenth century mills continued to be built here. Places such as Glossop and New Mills in Derbyshire and nearby Stalybridge and Marple in Cheshire, were transformed into industrial towns. Many mills remain, although they are now derelict or used for other purposes (Figure 64).

Many smaller post-medieval mills exist within the region, including disused corn-mills at Castleton, Bakewell, Alport and Hartington. The late nineteenth-century Cauldwells Mill at Rowsley, is the only one which still produces flour in the traditional way. Several paper-mills also existed, exploiting the pure water needed for manufacture, and ruined nineteenth-century examples survive at Crowden in Longdendale and Green's Mill, near North Lees, above Hathersage. A small bobbin-mill has been restored just west of Ashford. A nineteenth-century gunpowder-mill at Fernilee in the Goyt Valley, the only one in the region, now lies beneath the lower reservoir.

Rocks of many uses: quarries and their products

Domed millstones have been made in the Peak since at least the thirteenth century. These were quarried all along the gritstone escarpments of the eastern moors but with centres above Hathersage and Baslow. Each stone measures approximately 2m (6.5ft) across, with one flat face and one a low dome. By the sixteenth century Peak millstones were being shipped to the Thames estuary. In the seventeenth century, Peak stones were used throughout much of eastern and south-eastern England, trade reaching a peak at a time when superior continental stones were difficult to obtain due to political troubles abroad. The stones were taken eastwards overland and carried in barges from the river ports of Stainsforth and Bawtry. From Hull they went by ship to the Wash, the Thames estuary and south coast ports. In the eighteenth century the millstone trade all but collapsed. Continental stones again became available. Later the eating of white bread became fashionable. The Peak stones were unsuitable for making fine wheatflour as they turned it grey. While many of the main quarries above Hathersage have been reused in the nineteenth century, those above Baslow survive intact. They contain many unfinished stones, broken at various stages of production, both in the quarries and on the precipitous waste heaps. There is a complex series of access tracks, with ruined workmen's sheds, and the boulder-strewn slopes below the quarries contain many smaller delves and broken boulders where millstones have also been obtained (Figure 65).

In the nineteenth century several quarries, but those above Hathersage in particular, had a new lease of life, producing amongst other things millstones for animal food and pulpstones used for paper manufacture, many of which

FIGURE 65

Domed millstones at Gardom's Edge, above Baslow, abandoned during production. The stone in the foreground broke when nearly completed. The millstone maker's initials, denoting ownership, can be seen on the domed surface. The stone behind rests on the chock-stones placed beneath it to enable dressing to take place.

were exported to Scandinavia. Many of these can still be seen in the quarries, either broken during manufacture or stacked ready for sale. They are cylindrical in shape, with a flat edge. Most of the quarries closed in the late nineteenth or early twentieth centuries with the introduction of synthetic stones (Figure 66).

Many other gritstone quarries produced a variety of goods. Stone was quarried for building stone and for dressed items such as troughs, lintels and

FIGURE 66
Flat-edged millstones/pulpstones at Bole Hill Quarry above Hathersage. A large stack of stones remain at the side of a track, abandoned when millstone/pulpstone production stopped. This possibly occurred in 1901, when the quarry was purchased by Derwent Valley Water Board to provide stone for the Derwent and Howden Reservoirs, or after 1910, when the quarry may have been used again for a short period.

gateposts. Particularly good stone is still worked today around Stanton and Birchover. Other important quarries, now disused, include those on Fallange Edge above Rowsley, and on Cracken Edge above Chinley where the best stone was extracted by underground mining. The quarries at Hathersage were also used for building stone. One of these, the particularly large Bole Hill Quarry, was dug over only eight years to build two reservoir dams in the Upper Derwent valley (Figure 67).

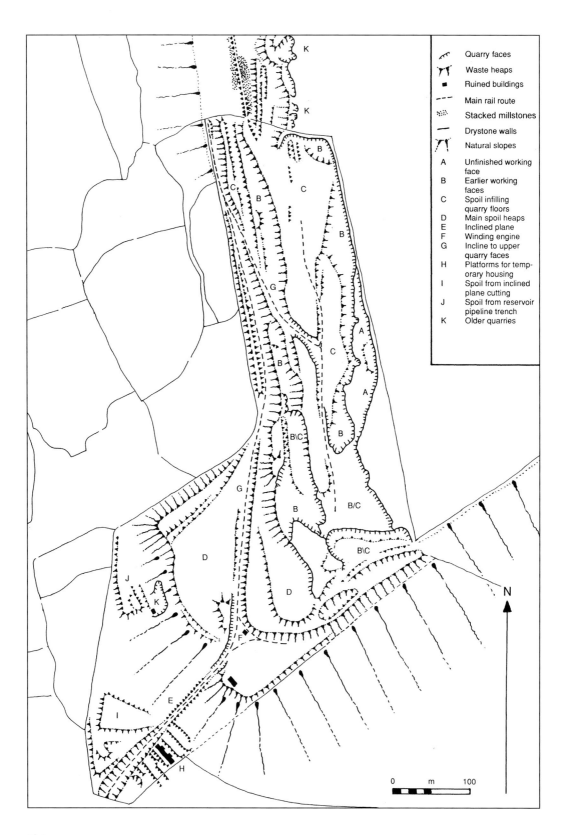

	Quarry faces
	Waste heaps
	Ruined buildings
	Main rail route
	Stacked millstones
	Drystone walls
	Natural slopes
A	Unfinished working face
B	Earlier working faces
C	Spoil infilling quarry floors
D	Main spoil heaps
E	Inclined plane
F	Winding engine
G	Incline to upper quarry faces
H	Platforms for temporary housing
I	Spoil from inclined plane cutting
J	Spoil from reservoir pipeline trench
K	Older quarries

0   m   100

N

Many dressed items were also made by breaking up surface boulders on the gritstone moors, a type of quarrying known as dayworking. Boulder-strewn areas still retain many signs of trough and lintel production, with the most suitable stones removed, leaving shallow pits surrounded by dressing waste, boulders with parts split away, and the occasional broken product.

Thinly bedded sandstones were quarried for flooring and roofing slabs. These quarries, comprising many shallow pits often covering relatively large areas, can be recognised on several moors.

The limestone plateau has traditionally also been a valuable source of stone. It makes a good building stone and the majority of local buildings and walls are built of it. Its other main traditional use is for the production of lime. Small-scale production by local farmers has been discussed in Chapter 7, but lime was also produced commercially. The first proto-industrial lime-burning centres grew up around Buxton and Bradwell. At the former there were kilns both at Grin Low south-west of the town, and at Dove Holes and Peak Forest to the north-east. At these three locations many circular limekilns survive, often close together, each with their own shallow quarry and waste heaps. Nothing appears to survive at Bradwell and this centre was perhaps short-lived. At Grin Low there are well over one hundred kilns of different sizes, dating from the seventeenth to mid-nineteenth centuries and these lie within a Country Park and can easily be inspected. The north-western part of the limestone plateau around Buxton had the advantage of available coal from nearby mines for burning the quarried limestone. In the mid-seventeenth century Dove Holes is recorded as having 14 kilns and by the second half of the eighteenth century lime was being produced in large quantities, particularly at Dove Holes, Grin Low and Peak Forest, but also at a series of smaller centres in the general vicinity. At first these kilns were rented to local individuals who supplemented other income by burning lime on an intermittent basis in summer months. In the mid-eighteenth century production was industrialised by the Devonshire Estate. They owned the land at Grin Low and Peak Forest, and from then on rented the kilns to professional limeburners, although this work was still seasonal, the kilns only operating in the summer half of the year (Figure 68).

At the turn of the nineteenth century the Dove Holes quarries rose to dominance with the building of the Peak Forest Tramway. This ran to the terminus of the Peak Forest canal at Buxworth Basin near Whaley Bridge, where impressive wharfs and kilns have been restored. It facilitated wide distribution of lime over much of the industrial north-west, for the chemical

FIGURE 67 (*opposite*)
Bole Hill Quarry above Hathersage. Although a much smaller millstone/pulpstone quarry existed here in the late nineteenth century, this quarry was largely dug between 1902 and 1910 for the 1.25 million tons of stone required to build the Derwent and Howden dams. Stone from the quarry face was taken down a zigzagged railway track, and then down an inclined plane. Near its foot was temporary housing for the quarry workers. At the bottom was the Midland Railway's Sheffield to Manchester line, which was used to take the stone up the Derwent Valley. From Bamford a purpose-built line led to the reservoirs.

and construction industries. Much of the burgeoning city of Manchester and its surrounding towns was built using lime-mortar made from the Dove Holes quarries, made in kilns along the canal and later also at the quarries. From this time lime was commonly produced industrially in banks of tall continuous-running kilns. Quarrying south of Buxton also increased dramatically after the

FIGURE 68

Limekilns at Dove Holes, near Buxton. This aerial view shows extensive limeworking, mostly dating from the seventeenth and eighteenth centuries. This was one of three major proto-industrial limeburning centres in this part of the Peak, supplying lime for industry and building to the growing city of Manchester and its environs, and to the general area for agricultural purposes. In the middle distance to the right, behind more-recent quarry waste heaps, can be seen the Neolithic Bull Ring henge.

opening of the Cromford and High Peak Railway in the 1830–31 and further quarries east of Buxton were developed with the building of the Midland Railway line through the Wye gorge in the 1860s. The particularly pure limestones in the general vicinity of Buxton make quarrying an important industry still. However, in this century large quarries have also been developed elsewhere, in the Hope Valley, around Wirksworth, and in the Weaver Hills west of Ashbourne.

The limestone plateau has also been the site of two minor quarrying industries of some interest. At Ashford, from medieval times until early in the twentieth century, an ornamental dark limestone known as Ashford Black Marble was quarried. There are extensive underground black marble mines near the west end of Ashford where parts of the mid-eighteenth-century mechanised dressing mill survives. Other decorative limestones were also quarried in the eighteenth and nineteenth centuries from elsewhere in the Peak. Chert, a hard stone similar to flint, found in beds within the limestone, was quarried and mined around Bakewell from the late eighteenth century. This was used in Staffordshire and Yorkshire potteries for grinding calcined flint, used in manufacturing as a whitening agent for the popular wares they mass-produced.

From rails to reservoirs: nineteenth- and twentieth-century additions to the landscape

The Peak District was little affected by the canal building of the eighteenth century which either skirted or stopped close to the edge of the region. In the 1790s the Peak Forest tramway was built, running from the quarries at Dove Holes to the impressive restored wharfs at the terminal of the Peak Forest Canal at Buxworth, near Whaley Bridge. In 1825 a much more ambitious scheme was started, to link the Peak Forest Canal, via the high limestone plateau, with the Cromford Canal to the south. The result, the Cromford and High Peak Railway, was opened in 1830–31. It was a considerable engineering achievement, with stationary steam engines at the top of inclined planes and cuttings and tunnels along its tortuous course. Originally wagons were pulled by horses, but steam locomotives were introduced in the 1830s. Closed in the 1960s, much of it is now a walking and cycle trail (Figure 69).

Main line links to the railway networks beyond the region entered the Peak in the mid-nineteenth century. The Midland line from Derby had come up the Derwent valley as far as Rowsley by 1848. In the 1860s it was taken through to Manchester, via the spectacular Wye valley gorge and a series of tunnels. The two other lines which crossed the region both connected Manchester with Sheffield. The Manchester, Sheffield and Lincolnshire Railway, later part of the LNER, built a line up Longdendale and through the Woodhead Tunnel, which opened in 1846. The Midland Railway eventually took a line through two long tunnels and the Hope and Edale valleys, which was not opened until the 1890s. This is the only main line still open (Figure 70).

FIGURE 69
The winding engine house at Middleton Top, near Wirksworth. This building contains the sole survivor of the eight winding engines on various inclines on the Cromford and High Peak Railway built between 1825 and 1829. This engine was made by the Butterley Iron Works in 1825 to pull trains up the 708-yard incline, which had a 1 in 8.25 gradient, on a continuous wire rope. It continued in use until 1963. The beam engine is still in place and can be seen working on several weekend through the year.

One activity of the nineteenth, twentieth and twenty-first centuries which has had minimal direct impact on the archaeological landscape is grouse shooting. The main structures are lines of shooting butts, built of stone, timber or turf in a variety of circular or rectangular designs. However, the turning over of moors to grouse-shooting in the early nineteenth century probably led to the survival of many important earlier archaeological remains. This is

FIGURE 70

The Midland Railway viaduct at Monsal Dale, near Longstone. This viaduct was built in the 1860s and was used by trains for a hundred years. It lay on the main line from London to Manchester. Since closure, the Wye Valley stretch, always noted for its spectacular views of the valley as the trains sped between tunnels, has been opened for walkers as the Monsal Trail. Currently there are plans to reopen the line but whether or not this succeeds remains to be seen.

particularly true on the eastern moors, with their nationally important pre-historic remains, where the dukes of Rutland and Devonshire held most of the land. Agricultural expansion in the nineteenth century would probably have been greater here if not for the sporting interest.

Of great impact in the remoter gritstone valleys was the creation of a series of reservoirs to provide water for the surrounding towns and cities. Sheffield

FIGURE 71

Mortar scars on rocks at Swine Sty, on Big Moor east of Baslow. Big Moor was used for training in the 1939–45 war
by the American Airborne Division and by the Home Guard. The rock outcrops were used for target practice and have
many scars created by rifle bullets and mortar bombs.

built its Redmires and Rivelin dams in the 1830s and 1840s, followed by those in the Loxley valley near Bradfield later in the century. Manchester built those in Longdendale between the 1840s and 1860s. The largest scheme, with massive stone-built dams, was the Derwent and Howden Reservoirs in the Upper Derwent valley. These were constructed in the early years of the twentieth century and an interesting associated site is the surviving building platforms of the planned navvy settlement at Birchenlee known locally as Tin Town. These dams were followed about 20 years later by the Ladybower Reservoir, built immediately downstream between 1935 and 1943. This involved the flooding of Derwent and Ashopton villages and much valuable farmland. A pipeline takes water down the Derwent valley to Leicester, Nottingham and Derby and a tunnel feeds Sheffield. Further twentieth-century developments have included the dams in the Goyt valley and recently that to the south of the region at Carsington (Colour Plate 16).

Preparing for conflict: wartime scars

The Peak District is not rich in relics of the 1914–18 and 1939–45 wars. High above Sheffield at Redmires there are silted trenches used for trench warfare training. The second war has left a variety of sites, including concrete pillboxes high on the hills south of Buxton around a large ammunition store, two built into prehistoric barrows, and searchlight battery earthworks in Edale and at Matlock. The eastern moors were used for military training and are littered with slit trenches and gun platforms, as well as unexploded munitions buried in the peat. These are found occasionally when soils are disturbed. Rock outcrops, prehistoric cairns and packhorse guidestones are peppered with bullet and mortar scars. The higher moorlands of the Peak contain several aircraft wrecks, although there is now little to see, as they have been extensively looted by souvenir hunters (Figure 71).

Today's Historic Landscape:
A Lasting Monument to the Past?

....

The layers of the onion: the present landscape and its origins in the past

To return to where we began, it was noted in the Introduction that the Peak landscape comprises a complex interleaving of features created by people over several millennia. Being predominantly upland in character, much remains visible, as destructive arable farming has had less impact when compared with the lowland zone. It is hoped that the chapters above have demonstrated that wherever we look, the landscape has been transformed by people and that there is great time depth to the many buildings, walls, hedges, fields, moorlands, routeways and industrial sites still in use today, as well as those earthworks more traditionally considered to be the preserve of the archaeologist. The Peak District is a particularly rich area, where the character of the present historic landscape changes with topography.

Both the limestone plateau and the main flanking valleys have been extensively used since earliest times. On the limestone plateau today's farmed landscape is largely defined in stone, with houses and outbuildings in white limestone surrounded by thousands of kilometres of field walls. Over the years, it has normally been easier to modify or add to the existing lay-out, into which so much labour has been invested in the past, rather than sweep it away and start again. Thus many of today's fields around villages have been in existence since medieval times. Others, on higher land, are very different in character and have been added over the last 300 or 400 years. Essentially, the present pattern of fields was established by the middle of the nineteenth century at the latest. The majority of the villages have existed in their present locations since at least medieval times. Although many of the stone dwellings and outbuildings have been built over the last 400 years, platforms which mark the sites of medieval timber farm-buildings can sometimes be seen in the spaces between the present structures. Beyond the villages the fields often contain dew ponds, small quarries with limekilns, and the hillocks of old lead mines. Although at any one time the vast majority of fields are used for pasture or as hay meadows, they have usually been ploughed in recent centuries and this has been sufficient to destroy much earlier surface evidence of human activity. However, earlier archaeological earthworks do survive. Sometimes this is because they were large monuments, like the Arbor Low henge or some barrows, whose destruction as part of normal agricultural activity was more trouble than it was worth. Additionally, some ceremonial monuments may have survived into the eighteenth or nineteenth centuries because superstition dictated that damage led to ill luck. Other sites survive on rocky ground, or on small shelves, where later cultivation has been inhibited. These include many barrows, and remains of Roman and possibly prehistoric settlements, and their fields (Figure 72).

Much that has been said about the limestone plateau also applies to the main valleys like the Derwent. However, field boundaries are sometimes hedged rather than walled and traditional field layouts have been easier to alter or remove. Virtually no monuments pre-dating the medieval period are known

FIGURE 72

Multi-period features on the limestone plateau around Sheldon. This aerial photograph shows enclosures of very different types: the narrow fields in the middle distance are the fossilised medieval open field of Sheldon, while the rectangular ones in the foreground were laid out after the 1767 Enclosure Award for Ashford. Crosscutting the agricultural features are lead mines, with Magpie Mine (Figure 62) prominent right of centre.

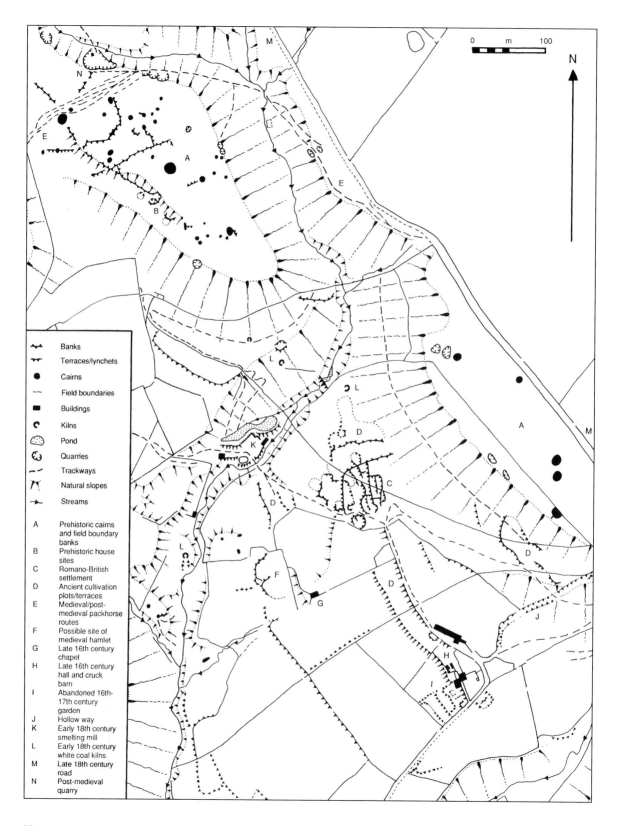

Banks

Terraces/lynchets

Cairns

Field boundaries

Buildings

Kilns

Pond

Quarries

Trackways

Natural slopes

Streams

A Prehistoric cairns and field boundary banks
B Prehistoric house sites
C Romano-British settlement
D Ancient cultivation plots/terraces
E Medieval/post-medieval packhorse routes
F Possible site of medieval hamlet
G Late 16th century chapel
H Late 16th century hall and cruck barn
I Abandoned 16th-17th century garden
J Hollow way
K Early 18th century smelting mill
L Early 18th century white coal kilns
M Late 18th century road
N Post-medieval quarry

as there are few significant topographical hindrances to cultivation. A notable exception is Chatsworth Park where barrows survive in the fossilised mid-eighteenth-century agricultural landscape with its extensive medieval strip earthworks and later field boundary banks. Extensive swathes of ridge and furrow and strip lynchets also survive around Bakewell and in the Peak's southern valleys (see Figure 50).

The gritstone uplands vary in character, with contrasts between the high moors to the north, the dissected ridges to the west and the continuous but lower moors to the east. This said, they also have elements in common. All have old roads and tracks, often visible as braided hollow-ways, which were the main communication routes before the laying out of the present road network in the eighteenth and nineteenth centuries. The eastern and western moors in particular have many abandoned coal mines and stone quarries.

The eastern moors are archaeologically the most important. They contain large tracts of prehistoric landscape, with farms, fields and monuments surviving here because the land has been little used except for upland grazing over the last two millennia. Between the surviving prehistoric complexes, destroying early features on the most favourable shelves, are farms with drystone-walled fields which date from the medieval period through to the nineteenth century (Figure 73).

The northern moors are very different. At their heart, because of their high altitude and deep peats, places like Kinder Scout and Bleaklow have relatively little visible archaeology. They are dissected by the deep valleys of the upper Derwent and its tributaries. Scattered farms, many dating back several hundred years, sit within a landscape of walled and hedged fields very different from that of the limestone plateau. Villages never developed along these narrow valleys. The valleys have been radically altered in the twentieth century with the building of reservoirs and large scale planting of conifers where there were once deciduous trees. Many of the steep valley sides are ancient woodlands once used for charcoal burning.

The western upland combines high moorland ridges with deep peat, that were too high for prehistoric farming, as on the northern moors, with lower enclosed areas covered with farms and the occasional village. Here the field patterns allow the growth of medieval and later intake to be plotted, with early self-contained farms being discernible from later infilling between them, a process completed in the nineteenth century.

FIGURE 73 (*opposite*)
A multi-period archaeological landscape around North Lees, near Hathersage. This landscape illustrates the richness of features on the eastern gritstone upland. The higher land to the north contains Bronze Age house platforms, clearance cairns, field boundaries and barrows, all within large nineteenth-century enclosures. In the valley below there is a multiperiod agricultural palimpsest, including a Romano-British settlement and a late sixteenth-century hall, with gardens which were abandoned when it later became a tenanted farm. The types of industrial activity also varied, and include an early eighteenth-century lead-smelting mill, with associated white coal kilns, and later stone quarrying. The mill was converted in the nineteenth century into a paper mill.

Awareness and legislation: protecting archaeological sites and the historic landscape for the future

Much of the Peak District lies within the National Park, which was created in 1951. This is an area of outstanding beauty surrounded by industrial cities, and is more heavily visited than any other National Park in Britain. The National Park Authority has two statutory responsibilities; to conserve the character of the Peak District landscapes and to enable visitors to enjoy them. It must also try to enable the local population to continue to earn its living within the Park. In many instances these aims are in conflict with each other and finding solutions often involves difficult balancing acts in order to care for the living landscape (Colour Plate 17).

The National Park Authority is also the planning authority and has powers over development that can be used to protect archaeological sites from destruction, both from new building and from mineral exploitation. The building of new roads and laying of pipelines are beyond its direct remit, as are everyday agricultural activities, although it does have some input into how these activities take place. Many of the most important archaeological sites in the region are given legal protection as Scheduled Monuments by the Secretary of State for Culture, Media and Sport and are managed indirectly by English Heritage. However, this approach is normally site-specific and this covers only a small percentage of sites. The vast majority of features that make up the historic landscape have no legal protection. This may be a good thing, for to go to the other extreme would lead to fossilisation of a dead landscape in which no-one could make a living. More appropriate are conservation measures which lead to voluntary conservation of the character of any given landscape in a dynamic way.

To counter undue depletion of the historic landscape – which in effect is the whole National Park, as there is no part of it which could be considered as a truly natural landscape – the National Park Authority has a range of positive conservation policies. Some of these are applied through the planning process, others rely on the dissemination of information on the value of given landscapes and features, and information on sensitive farming and land management practice. Liaison with national and regional bodies such as English Heritage, English Nature, the Countryside Agency, water companies and The National Trust have led to constructive partnerships. Liaison with local groups and societies is equally valuable. In order to pass on advice and assistance to farmers and other land managers, the holders of the final veto on whether most archaeological features survive or not and the true conservers of the character of the land, the National Park Authority has a Countryside and Economy Team. This team arranges specialist surveys and gives advice to farmers and others who express an interest in conservation. This often leads to agreements which ensure non-destructive management of the land.

As the number of visitors to the National Park increases this often exacerbates tensions between farmers and visitors. It is becoming increasingly common for people to go to archaeological sites marked on Ordnance Survey maps irrespective of whether there is public access or not. It is important that visitors realise that being within a National Park does not give them the freedom to roam at will over farmland. Those wanting to visit sites should keep to footpaths and open access land (as shown on Ordnance Survey Dark and White Peak Outdoor Leisure Maps). Visitors wanting to inspect sites on private land must first take the trouble of finding who farms the land and ask permission for access.

There are several professional archaeologists working on a permanent or regular basis in the region. The National Park Authority currently has a complement of seven, responsible for advising on management of the resource and for enhancing the known record of sites and landscapes, mainly through survey. Similarly, the areas outside the Park are covered by Local Authority Archaeologists, Sites and Monuments Record Officers, and Historic Environment Record Officers. English Heritage has Regional Inspectors of Ancient Monuments and Field Monument Wardens who are responsible for Scheduled Monuments. Excavations and other recording work is done regularly by archaeological contractors such as the Trent & Peak Archaeological Unit based at Nottingham University, and by ARCUS, their equivalent at Sheffield University. This is often only possible when funds are available because a site is to be developed. Increasingly such work is put out to tender and other archaeologists based elsewhere in the country compete for the work. Given the enhanced planning powers and the nature of the National Park landscape, large scale development is less common than many areas elsewhere in Britain. Research excavations are occasionally carried out by local universities, but in a time of scarce resources these are again often small scale. An exception was the extensive excavations undertaken at prehistoric features on Gardom's Edge between 1995 and 2000, a joint project by Sheffield University and the National Park Authority. Museums at Sheffield, Buxton, Derby and Stoke on Trent have professional staff responsible for the care and curation of artefacts found in the region. Amateur organisations active in the area include the Derbyshire Archaeological Society based in Derby, the Hunter Archaeological Society in Sheffield and ARTEAMUS based in the Peak District and South Yorkshire. Specialist interest groups include the Peak District Mines Historical Society who also run the Peak District Mining Museum at Matlock Bath, and Peak Rail, based at Matlock.

As noted above, it is farmers and landowners who are the main guardians of the archaeological resource. While the majority are not interested in archaeology as such, they often care greatly about what is on their land. Many features are destroyed not out of malice or from lack of care, but because it is not realised that features are of archaeological significance. Thus one of the most important tasks for the future is the identification and assessment of sites in the landscape and the passing of this information to farmers. In 2003 the National Park Authority had three professional survey archaeologists carrying out this work. This is far from an academic exercise, in that work done so far has demonstrated that substantial numbers of sites remain to be documented for the first time. However, the Park covers 555 square miles (1438 square kilometres), and it has been estimated that it will take over 35 years to cover the Park once. This task was started in-house in 1989 and is a bit like painting the Forth Road Bridge, in that there is continuing need to identify what still remains and what was missed the first time around. Given this, there is a very real role for the amateur archaeologist, recording sites within their local area or carrying out thematic surveys. Such archaeological work should always be carried out in liaison with professionals from the outset, to prevent duplication of effort and to ensure landowners are not subjected to an unwelcome surfeit of archaeologists.

Professional archaeologists involved in the management of the known archaeological resource in the region not only need to continue monitoring development, but increasingly need to be involved in managing the tensions between landowners and visitor pressure, as well as taking positive steps to ensure the balance is maintained between the impact of recreation and requirements of landscape conservation.

Perhaps the most important task for the future, for professionals and amateurs alike, is to continue the campaign to increase awareness of archaeology and the historic landscape. An increasing number of people who care about the conservation of, and research into, our archaeological heritage will lead to a more effective lobby for increasing funding, enhancing legislation and most importantly changing attitudes towards a positive view of what our past has to offer us, now and in the future.

Places to Visit

....

This short section lists a selection of the monuments described above that can be visited. All have public access unless stated. Please follow the Country Code as landowners may withdraw their co-operation if the Code is broken. This selection of sites is largely restricted to monuments in the countryside, and does not include many of the villages and monuments within them, which can easily be found on the accompanying map. Other omissions are stately homes and show caves and mines open to the public, details of which can be obtained from usual tourist information sources (Figure 74).

Prehistoric (Chapters 1–4)

Arbor Low henge and Gib Hill barrow (SK 160635) Approach from the Youlgreave to Parsley Hay road. Park up the track to Upper Oldhams Farm (SK 159637). A small access charge is made. A short walk from the farm to the henge, then on to the barrow in the adjacent field (see Figure 11, Colour Plates 2, 3, pp. 28, 30, 40).

Big Moor later prehistoric fields and ritual monuments (centred SK 275755) The extensive Open-Access moorland area west of the Baslow to Sheffield road has many prehistoric features as well as later hollow-ways and guide stones (see Figures 7, 8, 12, 17; pp. 19–23, 31, 39).

Bull Ring henge (SK 078782) A short walk from the main Buxton to Chapel en le Frith road to the henge, located next to the Dove Holes Community Centre and sports fields. Although not on a public footpath, there are no known access restrictions (see Figure 68, pp. 30, 40, 126).

Carl Wark hillfort (SK 260815) The easiest approach is from the south-west, a 1.5 km (0.9 miles) walk on paths across Open Access moorland, from a car park on the Sheffield to Hathersage road (SK 252801). Bole Hill and Lawrence Field are nearby (see below) (see Figures 18, 21, pp. 42–43, 46).

Five Wells chambered cairn (SK 124710) Park by the lane from Chelmorton to Fivewells Farms. A short walk, first along the green lane northwards, then along a signposted concessionary path running due east, leads to the monument. This is currently the only chambered cairn in the region with formal public access (see Figure 10; Colour Plate 1, pp. 27–29).

Gardom's Edge later prehistoric settlement and fields, and Neolithic enclosure (centred SK 275730) An extensive area between Gardom's and Birchen Edges has many prehistoric features typical of those on the eastern moors and also a large Neolithic enclosure. The moorland is Open Access land, but adjacent fields are private. There is a public car park on the Baslow to Chesterfield road near to the Robin Hood Inn (SK 280722), from where a circular walk can be made along footpaths, going above Gardom's Edge and returning under Birchen Edge (see Figure 4, pp. 9, 21, 23, 29, 38).

Hob Hurst's House (SK 287692) A walk from the road from Beeley to Chesterfield (SK 287681), following a rough walled lane north-westwards, over a tall gate and along a track

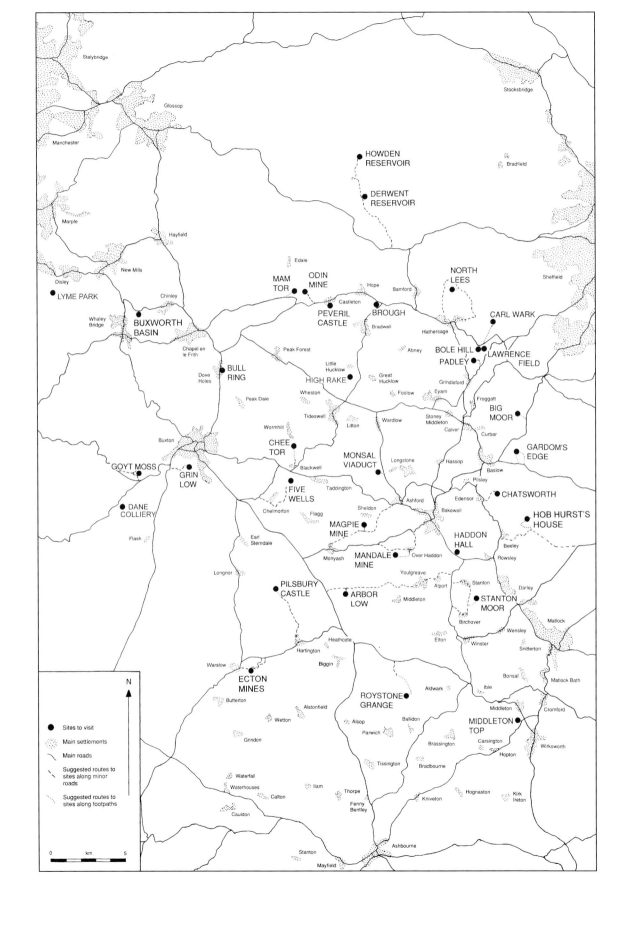

for about 30m and then a signed path north-eastwards to Harland Edge and ascends to this unusual barrow. A short distance further east, there are two packhorse guidestones near the path (see p. 33).

Mam Tor hillfort (SK 128836) A short but steep walk along footpaths from Mam Nick car park (SK 123832), on the Castleton to Chapel en le Frith road (via Winnats Pass) (see Figures 18, 19, pp. 42–45).

Stanton Moor stone circles, barrows and cairns (centred SK 248632) Roadside parking (SK 242628) on the road from Stanton to Birchover. Several well-used public footpaths cross the Open Access moorland (see Figure 16, pp. 37–38).

Roman (Chapter 4)

Brough Roman fort (SK 181827) A short signposted walk from roadside parking in Brough, a short distance after turning to Bradwell from the Hathersage to Hope road (see Figure 22; Colour Plate 7, pp. 46–48).

Chee Tor settlement (SK 127732) Although a public footpath passes close by, permission should be sought from Blackwell Hall Farm at Blackwell. The site is a 1km (0.6 miles) walk across fields from the farm. It can also be viewed from across the valley, as can ancient fields further east, from the Millers Dale to Wormhill road (see Figures 24, 25, 44, pp. 51–52, 86).

North Lees settlement (SK 234836) A 1 km (0.6 miles) walk along a track from the main car park (SK 238837) on the minor road following below Stanage Edge. Nearby, further along the same track, are the ruins of Green's Mill (SK 232836), once a paper mill and prior to that a lead smelting mill. On the way back a short detour along public footpaths leads to North Lees Hall (SK 235834), which can be viewed from the adjacent path (see Figure 73, pp. 51, 134).

Roystone Grange settlement (SK 200569) This site, together with the foundations of the medieval grange and several other features, forms part of the Roystone Grange Archaeological Trail. Leaflets describing the signposted route and features on it are obtainable from National Park Information Centres. The starting point is a car park on the High Peak Trail (SK 195581), off a minor road south from Pikehall, reached from the Cromford to Newhaven road (see Figures 5, 24, p. 50).

Medieval (Chapters 5–6, 8)

Lawrence Field settlement and enclosure (SK 253796) A short walk across Open Access moorland from a roadside car park (SK 252801) on the main road from Sheffield to Hathersage. There is a fine example of a deep hollow-way a short distance to the north between the road and the stream. Carl Wark and Bole Hill are nearby (see above) (see Figure 38, pp. 76–77, 92).

Padley Hall and Chapel (SK 246789) Leave the main Grindleford to Sheffield road in Nether Padley (SK 250785) towards Grindleford Station. Either park here and walk along a narrow and potholed road for just under 1km (0.6 miles) to the chapel, or park near here (see Figure 47, p. 91).

Peveril Castle (SK 149826) Park in Castleton. The castle is well signposted and is a short but steep climb. English Heritage make an admission charge (see Figure 30, Colour Plate 11, pp. 66, 91, 93).

FIGURE 74 (*opposite*)
The location of places to visit. This map gives the general location of each site. Ideally it should be used in conjunction with the Ordnance Survey 1:50,000 maps, or better still, their 1:25,000 Dark Peak and White Peak Explorer maps.

Pilsbury Castle (SK 114638) Drive (or walk) north from Hartington on a narrow gated road following the Dove valley. Very limited parking at Pilsbury. A short walk along a public footpath leads to the castle. There is currently concessionary access to the castle earthworks for visitors (see Figures 5, 37, 46, pp. 75, 89–90).

Roystone Grange – see above (see Figure 44, pp. 72, 76, 85–86, 92).

Packhorse Routes and Turnpikes (Chapter 10)

Big Moor hollow-ways and guidestones – see above (see Figure 56, pp. 105–106)

Lawrence Field hollow-way – see above (see Figure 55, p. 104).

Harland Edge guidestones – see above under Hob Hurst's House (see p. 106).

Derbyshire Bridge to Burbage turnpike road – see below under Goyt's Moss (see p. 110).

Industrial Sites (Chapter 11)

Bole Hill and Millstone Edge quarries (centred SK 249800) These lie on Open Access land to either side of the main road from Sheffield to Hathersage at Surprise View. There is car parking nearby (SK 252801). Care should be taken as all quarries are dangerous. Carl Wark and Lawrence Field (see above) are nearby (see Figures 66, 67, pp. 123–124).

Buxworth Basin (SK 022820) Parking at the site, off the minor road to Buxworth, from the B6062 from Chapel en le Frith via Chinley to Whaley Bridge. Alternatively walk along the canal from the wharf in the centre of Whaley Bridge (see pp. 125, 127).

Dane Colliery and Quarries (centred SK 010699) Limited roadside parking or walk from the Derbyshire Bridge car park (see Goyt Moss) along the main road to Congleton for about a mile (take care), until upslope of the colliery chimney. Various footpaths can be followed to pass close to the features of interest here, the main ones being the colliery chimney, the colliery adit (SK 008697) and the quarries on both sides of the stream (SK 013700/ SK 011698) (see Colour Plate 15, p. 117).

Derwent/Howden Reservoirs (SK 173898/SK 170924) A short walk from the Fairholmes car park (SK 173893) leads to the Derwent Reservoir dam. Nearby to the west are the remains of Tin Town navvy settlement. A drive further up the valley leads to the Howden Reservoir dam. This road is closed to cars above Fairholmes at weekends, but can be reached by bus or bicycle (see Colour Plate 16, p. 131).

Ecton Mines (centred SK 100581) Park at laneside parking at the base of the hill to the west side (SK 096582) or walk from Hulme End on the Manifold Way trail. Various footpaths criss-cross the hill and go past extensive mine workings and buildings. The Boulton and Watt engine house is on the ridgetop close to paths via the Folly, the building with a green spire on the hillside a short distance north of the parking place (see pp. 49, 116–117).

Goyt Moss coal mines (centred SK 019715) The Derbyshire Bridge car park, on a minor road at the head of the Goyt Valley and a short distance off the main Buxton to Macclesfield road, is at the heart of the colliery. All lie within Open Access moorland and several shafts to the south lie adjacent to public paths and tracks. The disused walled lane running north-eastwards is a disused eighteenth-century turnpike road. Care should be taken, as many of the run-in shafts contain deep pools of water, while it is not advised to stand in the hollows of others as there is always a possibility that the shafts may reopen (see Figure 63, pp. 117–119).

Grin Low limekilns (centred SK 054717) Park in the public car park (SK 048720) in Grin Low quarry adjacent to the caravan park. This is approached from the back road to Harpur Hill, shortly after leaving the main Buxton to Leek road. A short walk leads to Solomon's Temple, built on a barrow, on the hilltop (SK 054717). This is surrounded by limekilns and quarries. Further examples can be found in the woods between here and Pooles Cavern (SK 049725).

Here there is a small museum with information on the lime industry and Romano-British finds from the cave. The whole of the route described is within country parks with public paths (see p. 125).

High Rake Mine and Tideslow Rake (SK 164778/SK 155779) Limited parking on the lane running west from Windmill (SK 166778), or park in Great Hucklow. Follow the track westwards to High Rake Mine, currently being restored by the Peak District Mines Historical Society, and continue on to the public footpath along Tideslow Rake (see Colour Plate 17, p. 114).

Magpie Mine (SK 172682) Roadside parking, at the entrance to the track to the mine, on the minor road from Ashford to Monyash. The mine buildings are obvious from the road and are only a short walk down the access track (see Figures 62, 72, pp. 114–115, 133).

Mandale Mine (SK 194661) Park on the narrow lane from Over Haddon to Lathkill Dale (SK 203662). A 1km (0.6 miles) walk up Lathkill Dale leads to the stone-lined sough tail next to the main path. The engine house is set back in trees a short distance above the sough tail (see p. 114).

Middleton Top Engine House (SK 275552) Drive to the visitor centre here following a signposted lane from Middleton by Wirksworth, off the Carsington Road. It is located at the top of an impressive incline on the High Peak Trail, which is an alternative access route (see Figure 69, p. 128).

Monsal Dale Viaduct (SK 182716) Park at Monsal Head, on the Ashford to Wardlow road. A short but steep signposted path leads down to the viaduct (see Figure 70, p. 129).

North Lees Hall and Green's Mill – see above under North Lees settlement (see Figure 73, Colour Plate 13, pp. 98, 121, 134).

Odin Mine (SK 134835) Park at the end of the public road from Castleton to the base of Mam Tor. The open cut into the vein is immediately to the west of the road. The crushing circle and shafts are below the road to the east (see p. 114).

Many archaeological artefacts from the region are on display in Buxton Museum, downhill from the market place, and in Sheffield City Museum, located in Weston Park near the main University Campus. The Peak District Mining Museum, in the Pavilion at Matlock Bath, displays lead mining exhibits and opens Temple Mine nearby.

Bibliography

....

The Peak District

General

Anderson, P. and Shimwell, D. (1981) *Wild Flowers and Other Plants of the Peak District.* Ashbourne: Moorland.

Cameron, K. (1959) *The Place-Names of Derbyshire* (3 vols). Cambridge: Cambridge University Press.

Currie, C. R. J. (1996) *The Victoria History of the County of Stafford Volume VII: Leek and the Moorlands.* Oxford: Oxford University Press.

Edwards, K. C. (1990) The Peak District (3rd edn). London: Bloomsbury.

Elringham, C. R. (ed.) (1986) *A History of the County of Chester.* London: Victoria County Histories.

Ford, T. D. (2002) *Rocks and Scenery of the Peak District.* Ashbourne: Landmark.

Hart, C. R. (1981) *The North Derbyshire Archaeological Survey.* Chesterfield: North Derbyshire Archaeological Trust.

Heath, J. (1993) *An Illustrated History of Derbyshire.* Derby: Breedon Books.

Hodges, R. (1991) *Wall-to-Wall History: the Story of Roystone Grange.* London: Duckworth.

Hodges, R. and Smith, K. (eds) (1991) *Recent Developments in the Archaeology of the Peak District.* Sheffield: University of Sheffield.

Neves, R. and Downie, C. (eds) (1967) *Geological Excursions in the Sheffield Region and the Peak District National Park.* Sheffield: University of Sheffield.

Phillips, A. D. M. and Phillips, C. D. (2002) *A New Historical Atlas of Cheshire.* Chester: Cheshire County Council and Cheshire Community Council Publications Trust.

Smith, R. and Manley, R. (2000) *The Peak District: The Official National Park Guide.* Newton Abbot: David and Charles.

Turbutt, G. (1999) *A History of Derbyshire* (4 vols). Whitchurch: Merton Priory Press.

Prehistory (Chapters 1–4)

Ainsworth, S. (2001) Prehistoric settlement remains on the Derbyshire gritstone moors. *Derbyshire Archaeological Journal* 121: 19–69.

Ainsworth, S. and Barnatt, J. (1998) A scarp-edge enclosure at Gardom's Edge, Baslow, Derbyshire. *Derbyshire Archaeological Journal* 118: 5–23.

Ashbee, P. and Ashbee, R. (1981) A cairn on Hindlow, Derbyshire: Excavations 1953. *Derbyshire Archaeological Journal* 101: 9–41.

Barnatt, J. (1986) Bronze Age remains on the East Moors of the Peak District. *Derbyshire Archaeological Journal* 106: 18–100.

Barnatt, J. (1987) Bronze Age settlement on the gritstone East Moors of the Peak District of Derbyshire and South Yorkshire. *Proceedings of the Prehistoric Society* 53: 393–418.

Barnatt, J. (1990) *The Henges, Stone Circles and Ringcairns of the Peak District.* Sheffield: University of Sheffield, Sheffield Archaeological Monographs 1.

Bibliography

Barnatt, J. (1993) *Haddon Park, Nether Haddon, Derbyshire: Archaeological Survey 1993.* Unpublished report. Bakewell: Peak District National Park Authority Archaeology Service archive.

Barnatt, J. (1994) Excavation of a Bronze Age unenclosed cemetery, cairns and field boundaries at Eaglestone Flat, Curbar, Derbyshire, 1984, 1989–90. *Proceedings of the Prehistoric Society* 60: 287–370.

Barnatt, J. (1996) Moving between the monuments: Neolithic land use in the Peak District. In P. Frodsham (ed.) *Neolithic Studies in No-Man's Land: Papers on the Neolithic of Northern England, from the Trent to the Tweed.* Northern Archaeology, Volume 13/14: 45–62.

Barnatt, J. (1996) Recent research at Peak District stone circles; including restoration work at Barbrook II and Hordron Edge and new fieldwork elsewhere. *Derbyshire Archaeological Journal* 116: 27–48.

Barnatt, J. (1996) A multiphased barrow at Liffs Low, near Biggin, Derbyshire. In J. Barnatt and J. Collis (eds) *Barrows in the Peak District: Recent Research.* Sheffield: University of Sheffield.

Barnatt, J. (1996) *Arbor Low: A Guide to the Monuments.* Bakewell: Peak National Park.

Barnatt, J. (1998) Monuments in the landscape: thoughts from the Peak. In A. Gibson (ed.) *Prehistoric Ritual and Religion: Essays in Honour of Aubrey Burl.* Stroud: Sutton Publishing.

Barnatt, J. (1999) Taming the land: Peak District farming and ritual in the Bronze Age. *Derbyshire Archaeological Journal* 119: 19–78.

Barnatt, J. (2000) To each their own: Later Prehistoric farming communities and their monuments in the Peak. *Derbyshire Archaeological Journal* 120: 1–86.

Barnatt, J., Bevan, B. and Edmonds, M. (2001) A time and place for enclosure: Gardom's Edge, Derbyshire. In T. Darvill and J. Thomas (eds) *Neolithic Enclosures in Altantic Northwest Europe.* Oxford: Oxbow.

Barnatt, J., Bevan, B. and Edmonds, M. (2002) Gardom's Edge: a landscape through time. *Antiquity* 76: 50–56.

Barnatt, J. and Collis, J. (1996) *Barrows in the Peak District: Recent Research.* Sheffield: University of Sheffield.

Barnatt, J. and Edmonds, M. (2002) Places apart? Caves and monuments in Neolithic and Earlier Bronze Age Britain. *Cambridge Archaeological Journal* 12.1: 113–129.

Barnatt, J. and Reeder, P. (1982) Prehistoric rock art in the Peak District. *Derbyshire Archaeological Journal* 102: 33–44.

Barnatt, J. and Robinson, F. (2003) Prehistoric rock art at Ashover School and further new discoveries in the Peak District. *Derbyshire Archaeological Journal* 123: 1–28.

Bateman, T. (1848) *Vestiges of the Antiquities of Derbyshire.* London.

Bateman, T. (1861) *Ten Years Diggings in Celtic and Saxon Grave Hills in the Counties of Derby, Stafford and York.* London and Derby.

Bramwell, D. (1973) *Archaeology in the Peak District: a Guide to the Region's Prehistory.* Hartington: Moorland.

Clough, T. H. McK, and Cummins, W. A. (eds) (1988) *Stone Axe Studies, Volume 2: The Petrology of Prehistoric Stone Implements from the British Isles.* London: Council of British Archaeology Research Report No. 67.

Collis, J. (1983) *Wigber Low, Derbyshire: A Bronze Age and Anglian Burial Site in the White Peak.* Sheffield: University of Sheffield.

Coombs, D. G. and Thompson, F. H. (1979) Excavations of the hill fort of Mam Tor, Derbyshire 1965–69. *Derbyshire Archaeological Journal* 99: 7–51.

Edmonds, M. and Seaborne, T. (2001) *Prehistory in the Peak.* Stroud: Tempus.

Hart, C. R. and Makepeace, G. A. (1993) 'Cranes Fort', Conksbury, Youlgreave, Derbyshire: A newly discovered hillfort. *Derbyshire Archaeological Journal* 113: 16–20.

Heathcote, J. P. (1930) Excavations at barrows on Stanton Moor. *Derbyshire Archaeological Journal* 51: 1 44.

Heathcote, J. P. (1936) Further excavations on Stanton Moor. *Derbyshire Archaeological Journal* 57: 21–42.

Heathcote, J. P. (1939) Excavations on Stanton Moor. *Derbyshire Archaeological Journal* 60: 105–15.

Heathcote, J. P. (1954) Excavations on Stanton Moor. *Derbyshire Archaeological Journal* 74: 128–33.

Hicks, S. P. (1972) The impact of man on the East Moors of Derbyshire from Mesolithic times. *Derbyshire Archaeological Journal* 129: 1–21.

Kitchen, W. H. (2000) *Later Neolithic and Bronze Age land use and settlement in the Peak District: Cairnfields in context.* Unpublished Ph.D thesis, University of Sheffield.

Long, D. J., Chambers, F. M. and Barnatt, J. (1998) The palaeoenvironment and the vegetation history of a later prehistoric field system at Stoke Flat on the gritstone uplands of the Peak District. *Journal of Archaeological Science* 25: 505–519.

Makepeace, G. A. (1999) Cratcliff Rocks – A Forgotten Hillfort. *Derbyshire Archaeological Journal* 119: 12–18.

Marsden, B. M. (1963) The re-excavation of the Green Low, a Bronze Age barrow on Alsop Moor, Derbyshire. *Derbyshire Archaeological Journal* 83: 82–89.

Marsden, B. M. (1970) The excavation of the Bee Low round cairn, Youlgreave. *Antiquaries Journal* 50: 186–215.

Marsden, B. M. (1976) The excavation of Snelslow and Lean Low round cairns, Derbyshire. *Derbyshire Archaeological Journal* 96: 5–14.

Marsden, B. M. (1982) Excavations at the Minninglow Chambered Cairn (Ballidon 1), Ballidon, Derbyshire. *Derbyshire Archaeological Journal* 102: 8–22.

Morgan, V. and Morgan, P. (2001) *Rock Around the Peak.* Wilmslow: Sigma.

Wilson, A. and Barnatt, J. (in press) Excavation of a prehistoric clearance cairn and ritual pits on Sir William's Hill, Eyam Moor, Derbyshire, 2000. *Derbyshire Archaeological Journal* 124.

Wilson, J. and English, E. (1998) Investigation of a ditch and bank at Fin Cop at Monsal Head, Ashford, Derbyshire. *Derbyshire Archaeological Journal* 118: 86–93.

Roman (Chapter 4)

Barnatt, J. (1999) Prehistoric and Roman mining in the Peak District: Present knowledge and future research. *Mining History* 14.2: 19–30.

Barnatt, J. and Thomas, G. H. (1998) Prehistoric mining at Ecton, Staffordshire: A dated antler tool and its context. *Mining History* 13.5: 51–64.

Bevan, B. (2000) *Peak District Romano-British Rural Upland Settlement Survey 1998–2000.* Unpublished report. Bakewell: Peak District National Park Authority Archaeology Service archive.

Chadwick, A. M. and Evans, H. (2000) Reading Roystone's rocks: Landscape survey and lithic analysis from test pitting at Roystone Grange, Ballidon Derbyshire, and its implications for previous interpretation of the region. *Derbyshire Archaeological Journal* 120: 101–122.

Dearne, M. J., Anderson, S. and Branigan, K. (1995) Excavations at Brough Field, Carsington, 1980. *Derbyshire Archaeological Journal* 115: 37–75.

Guilbert, G. (1996) The oldest artefact of lead in the Peak: new evidence from Mam Tor. *Mining History* 13.1: 12–18.

Hodges, R. and Wildgoose, M. (1981) Roman or native in the White Peak: the Roystone Grange Project and its regional implications. *Derbyshire Archaeological Journal* 101: 42–57.

Jones, G. D. B. (1967) Manchester University Excavations, Brough on Noe (Navio) 1967. *Derbyshire Archaeological Journal* 87: 154–58.

Jones, G. D. B. and Wild, J. P. (1968) Excavation at Brough on Noe (Navio) 1986. *Derbyshire Archaeological Journal* 88: 89–93.

Ling, R. and Courtney, T. (1981) Excavations at Carsington, 1979–80. *Derbyshire Archaeological Journal* 101: 58–87.

Bibliography

Ling, R., Hunt, C. O., Manning, W. H., Wild, F. and Wild, J. P. (1990) Excavations at Carsington, 1983–84. *Derbyshire Archaeological Journal* 110: 30–55.

Makepeace, G. A. (1998) Romano-British rural settlements in the Peak District and north-east Staffordshire. *Derbyshire Archaeological Journal* 118: 95–138.

Stanley, J. (1954) An Iron Age fort at Ball Cross Farm, Bakewell. *Derbyshire Archaeological Journal* 74: 85–99.

Wroe, P. (1982) Roman roads in the Peak District. *Derbyshire Archaeological Journal* 102: 49–73.

Early Medieval (Chapter 5)

Barnatt, J. and Myers, A. M. (1984) Pre-Norman cross fragments from Monyash, Derbyshire. *Derbyshire Archaeological Journal* 104: 5–9.

Roffe, D. (1986) *The Derbyshire Domesday.* Darley Dale: Derbyshire Museums Service.

Sharpe, N. T. (2002) *Crosses of the Peak District.* Ashbourne: Landmark.

Sidebottom, P. C. (1999) Stone crosses in the Peak and 'the sons of Eadwulf'. *Derbyshire Archaeological Journal* 119: 206–219.

Stafford, P. (1985) *The East Midlands in the Early Middle Ages.* Leicester: Leicester University Press.

Stetka, J. (2001) *From Fort to Field: The Shaping of the Landscape of Bakewell in the 10th Century.* Privately Published.

Medieval/Post-Medieval Settlement and Farming (Chapters 6–9)

Barnatt, J. (1997) *Chatsworth Park: Archaeological Survey 1996–7.* Bakewell: Unpublished report for the Trustees of the Chatsworth Settlement and English Heritage. Bakewell: Peak District National Park Authority Archaeology Service archive.

Barnatt, J. (2002) *The Bakewell Archaeological Survey 2002.* Unpublished report. Bakewell: Peak District National Park Authority Archaeology Service archive.

Brighton, T. (1995) Chatsworth's sixteenth-century parks and gardens. *Garden History* 23.1: 29–55.

Burton, I. E. (1966) *The Royal Forest of the Peak.* Bakewell: Peak Park Planning Board.

Carr, J. P. (1963) Open field agriculture in mid-Derbyshire. *Derbyshire Archaeological Journal* 83: 66–76.

Craven, M. and Stanley, M. (2001) *The Derbyshire Country House* (3rd edn, 2 vols). Ashbourne: Landmark.

Hawkins, A. and Rumble, A. (1976) *Domesday Book: Staffordshire.* Chichester: Phillimore.

Hodges, R., Poulter, M. and Wildgoose, M. (1982) The medieval grange at Roystone. *Derbyshire Archaeological Journal* 102: 88–100.

Hodges, R. and Wildgoose, M. (1991) Roystone Grange: Excavations of the Cistercian Grange 1980–87. *Derbyshire Archaeological Journal* 111: 46–50.

Jackson, J. C. (1962) Open field cultivation in Derbyshire. *Derbyshire Archaeological Journal* 82: 54–72.

Joyce, B., Michell, G. and Williams, M. (1996) *Derbyshire. Detail and Character.* Alan Sutton Publishing Ltd.

Leach, J. T. (1995) Burning lime in Derbyshire pye kilns. *Industrial Archaeology Review* 17.2: 145–158.

Leonard, J. (1993) *Derbyshire Parish Churches from the Eighth to Eighteenth Centuries.* Derby: Breedon Books.

Morgan, P. (1978) *Domesday Book: Derbyshire.* Chichester: Phillimore.

Pevsner, N. (1975) *The Buildings of England: Staffordshire* (2nd edn). Harmondsworth: Penguin.

Pevsner, N. (1978) *The Buildings of England: Derbyshire* (2nd edn). Harmondsworth: Penguin.

Salter, M. (1998) *The Old Parish Churches of Derbyshire.* Malvern: Folly.

Wightman, W. E. (1961) Open field agriculture in the Peak District. *Derbyshire Archaeological Journal* 81: 111–125.

Wildgoose, M. (1991) The drystone walls of Roystone Grange. *Archaeological Journal* 148: 205–40.

Medieval/Post-Medieval Roads (Chapter 10)

Barnatt, J. (1993) *Edale Valley: Archaeological Survey 1993.* Unpublished report. Bakewell: Peak
District National Park Authority Archaeology Service archive.

Dodd A. E. and Dodd, E. M. (1980) *Peakland Roads and Trackways* (2nd edn) Ashbourne:
Moorland.

Hey, D. (1980) *Packmen, Carriers and Packhorse Roads.* Leicester: Leicester University Press.

Radley, J. (1963) Peak District roads prior to the turnpike era. *Derbyshire Archaeological Journal*
83: 39–50.

Radley, J. and Penny, S. R. (1972) The turnpike roads of the Peak District. *Derbyshire
Archaeological Journal* 92: 93–109.

Roberts, A. F. (1992) *Turnpike Roads Around Buxton.* Privately published.

Smith, H. (1996) *The Guide Stoops of Derbyshire.* Privately published.

Medieval/Post-Medieval Industry (Chapter 11)

Barnatt, J. (2002) The development of the Deep Ecton Mine, Staffordshire, 1723–1760. *Mining
History* 15.1: 10–23.

Barnatt, J. and Dickson, A. (in press) Survey and interpretation of an early limeburning complex
at Peak Forest, Derbyshire. *Derbyshire Archaeological Journal 124.*

Barnatt, J. and Leach, J. (1997) The Goyt's Moss Colliery, Buxton. *Derbyshire Archaeological
Journal* 117: 56–80.

Barnatt, J. and Rieuwerts, J. (1998) The Upper Nestus Pipes: an ancient lead mine in the Peak
District of Derbyshire. *Mining History* 13.5: 51–64.

Bowering, G. and Flindall, R. (1998) Hard times: A history of the Derbyshire chert industry.
Mining History 13.5: 1–33.

Cooper, B. (1991) *Transformation of a Valley: the Derbyshire Derwent.* Cromford: Scarthin.

Crossley, D. and Kiernan, D. (1992) The lead smelting mills of Derbyshire. *Derbyshire
Archaeological Journal* 112: 6–47.

Ford, T. D. (2000) *Derbyshire Blue John.* Ashbourne: Landmark.

Ford, T. D. and Rieuwerts, J. H. (2000) *Lead Mining in the Peak District* (4th edn). Matlock
Bath: Peak District Mines Historical Society.

Harris, H. (1971) *Industrial Archaeology of the Peak District.* Newton Abbot: David and Charles.

Hodgkins, D. J. (1987) The Peak Forest Canal – lime and limestone 1794–1846. *Derbyshire
Archaeological Journal* 107: 73–91.

Hopkinson, G. G. (1957) The development of the South Yorkshire and North Derbyshire
coalfield, 1500–1775. *Transactions of the Hunter Archaeological Society* 7.6: 295–319.

Hudson, B. (1989) *Through Limestone Hills: the Peak Line – Ambergate to Chinley.* Sparkford:
Oxford Publishing.

Kiernan, D. (1989) *The Derbyshire Lead Industry in the Sixteenth Century.* Chesterfield:
Derbyshire Record Society, Vol. 14.

Kiernan, D. and Van de Noort, R. (1992) Bole smelting in Derbyshire. In L. Willies and D.
Cranstone (eds) *Boles and Smeltmills: Report of a Seminar on the History and Archaeology of
Lead Smelting held at Reath, Yorkshire, 15–17 May 1992.* Historical Metallurgy Society Ltd.

Leach, J. T. (1996) Grin Hill, Buxton: A major Derbyshire limestone quarry. *Derbyshire
Archaeological Journal* 116: 101–134.

Polak, J. P. (1987) The production and distribution of Peak millstones from the sixteenth to the
eighteenth centuries. *Derbyshire Archaeological Journal* 107: 55–72.

Porter, L. and Robey, J. (2000) *The Copper and Lead Mines around the Manifold Valley, North
Staffordshire.* Ashbourne: Landmark.

Rieuwerts, J. H. (1987) *History and Gazetteer of the Lead Mine Soughs of Derbyshire.* Sheffield:
Privately published.

Rieuwerts, J. H. (1998) *Glossary of Derbyshire Lead Mining Terms.* Matlock Bath: Peak District
Mines Historical Society.

Ripley, D. (1989) *The Peak Forest Tramway.* Oxford: Oakwood Press.

Bibliography

Robinson, B. (1993) *Walls Across the Valley: The Building of the Howden and Derwent Dams.* Cromford: Scarthin Books.

Rimmer, A. (1985) *The Cromford and High Peak Railway.* Oxford: Oakwood Press.

Roberts, A. F. and Leach, J. R. (1985) *The Coal Mines of Buxton.* Cromford: Scarthin Books.

Tomlinson, J. M. (1996) *Derbyshire Black Marble.* Matlock Bath: Peak District Mines Historical Society.

Tucker, G. (1985) Millstone making in the Peak District of Derbyshire: the quarries and the technology. *Industrial Archaeology Review* 8.1: 42–58.

Willies, L. (1990) Derbyshire Lead Smelting in the eighteenth and nineteenth centuries. *Bulletin of the Peak District Mines Historical Society* 11.1: 1–19.

Willies, L. and Parker, H. (1999) *Peak District Mining and Quarrying.* Stroud: Tempus.

Wood, A. (1999) *The Politics of Social Conflict: The Peak Country 1520–1770.* Cambridge: Cambridge University Press.

Selected background reading

General

Foster, S. and Smout, T. C. (eds) (1994) *The History of Soils and Field Systems.* Aberdeen: Scottish Cultural Press.

Evans, J. G. (1999) *Land and Archaeology: Histories of Human Environment in the British Isles.* Stroud: Tempus.

Hunter, J. and Ralston, I. (eds) (1999) *The Archaeology of Britain: An Introduction from the Upper Palaeolithic to the Industrial Revolution.* London: Routledge.

Johnson, M. (1999) *Archaeological Theory: An Introduction.* Oxford: Blackwell.

Jones, M. (1986) *England Before Domesday.* London: Batsford.

Rackham, O. (1986) *The History of the Countryside.* London: Dent

Simmons, I. G. (2001) *An Environmental History of Great Britain: From 10,000 Years Ago to the Present.* Edinburgh: Edinburgh University Press.

Taylor, C. (1975) *Fields in the English Landscape.* London: Dent.

Prehistory (Chapters 1–4)

Barrett, J. C. (1994) *Fragments from Antiquity: an Archaeology of Social Life in Britain, 2900–1200 BC.* Oxford: Blackwell.

Beckensall, S. (1999) *British Prehistoric Rock Art.* Stroud: Tempus.

Bevan, B. (ed.) (1999) *Northern Exposure: Interpretative Devolution and the Iron Ages in Britain.* Leicester: University of Leicester.

Bewley, R. (2003) *Prehistoric Settlements.* Stroud: Tempus.

Bradley, R. (1984) *The Social Foundations of Prehistoric Britain.* London: Longman.

Bradley, R. (1993) *Altering the Earth.* Edinburgh: Society of Antiquaries of Scotland.

Bradley, R. (1998) *The Significance of Monuments.* London: Routledge.

Bruck, J. (ed.) (2001) *Bronze Age Landscapes: Tradition and Transformation.* Oxford: Oxbow.

Bruck, J. and Goodman, M. (eds) (1999) *Making Places in the Prehistoric World.* Cambridge: University of Cambridge.

Burgess, C. (1980) *The Age of Stonehenge.* London: Dent.

Burl, A. (2000) *The Stone Circles of Britain, Ireland and Brittany.* New Haven and London: Yale University Press.

Clarke, D. V., Cowie, T. G. and Foxon, A. (1985) *Symbols of Power at the Time of Stonehenge.* Edinburgh: HMSO.

Cunliffe, B. (1991) *Iron Age Communities in Britain* by Barry Cunliffe (3rd edn). London: Routledge.

Cunliffe, B. (ed.) (1994) *The Oxford Illustrated Prehistory of Europe.* Oxford: Oxford University Press.

Darvill, T. and Thomas, J. (eds) (2001) *Neolithic Enclosures in Atlantic Northwest Europe.* Oxford: Oxbow.

Edmonds, M. (1999) *Ancestral Geographies of the Neolithic: Landscapes, Monuments and Memory.* London: Routledge.

Oswald, A., Dyer, C. and Barber, M. (2001) *The Creation of Monuments: Neolithic causewayed enclosures in the British Isles.* Swindon: English Heritage.

Parker-Pearson, M. (1993) *Bronze Age Britain.* London: Batsford.

Pitts, M. and Roberts, M. (1997) *Fairweather Eden.* London: Century.

Pryor, F. (1998) *Farmers in Prehistoric Britain.* Stroud: Tempus.

Pryor, F. (2003) *Britain* BC*: Life in Britain and Ireland before the Romans.* London: Harper Collins.

Tilley, C. (1994) *A Phenomenology of Landscape: Places, Paths and Monuments.* Oxford: Berg.

Thomas, J. (1999) *Understanding the Neolithic.* London: Routledge.

Woodward, A. (2000) *British Barrows: A Matter of Life and Death.* Stroud: Tempus.

Roman (Chapter 4)

Frere, S. S. (1987) *Britannia: A History of Roman Britain* (3rd edn). London: Routledge.

Hingley, R. (1989) *Rural Settlement in Roman Britain.* London: Seaby.

Millet, M. (1990) *The Romanization of Britain.* Cambridge: Cambridge University Press.

Salway, P. (1993) *The Oxford Illustrated History of Roman Britain.* Oxford: Oxford University Press.

Medieval/Post-Medieval (Chapters 5–11)

Astill, G. and Grant, A. (eds) (1988) *The Countryside of Medieval England.* Oxford: Blackwell.

Beckett, J. V. (1988) *The East Midlands from* AD *1000.* London: Longman.

Brunskill, R. W. (1978) *Illustrated Handbook of Vernacular Architecture* (2nd edn). London: Faber and Faber.

Clarke, H. (1984) *The Archaeology of Medieval England.* London: Colonnade.

Crossley, D. (1990) *Post-Medieval Archaeology in Britain.* Leicester: Leicester University Press.

Hinton, D. A. (1990) *Archaeology, Economy and Society: England from the Fifth to the Fifteenth Century.* London: Seaby.

James, N. D. G. (1981) *A History of English Forestry.* Oxford: Blackwell.

Johnson, M. (1996) *An Archaeology of Capitalism.* Oxford: Blackwell.

Lewis, C., Mitchell-Fox, P. and Dyer, C. (2001) *Village, Hamlet and Field: Changing Medieval Settlements in Central England.* Bollington: Windgather Press.

Newman, R. (2001) *The Historical Archaeology of Britain, c. 1540–1900.* Stroud: Sutton.

Palmer, M. and Neaverson, P. (1998) *Industrial Archaeology: Principles and Practice.* London: Routledge.

Platt, C. (1978) *Medieval England.* London: Routledge.

Richards, J. D. (1991) *Viking Age England.* London: Batsford.

Roberts, B. K. and Wrathmell, S. (2000) *An Atlas of Rural Settlement in England.* London: English Heritage.

Taigel, A. and Williamson, T. (1993) *Parks and Gardens.* London: Batsford.

Wade Martins, S. (1991) *Historic Farm Buildings.* London: Batsford.

Wade Martins, S. (1995) *Farms and Fields.* London: Batsford.

Welch, M. (1992) *Anglo-Saxon England.* London: Batsford.

Williamson, T. (1995) *Polite Landscapes: Gardens and Society in Eighteenth Century England.* Stroud: Sutton.

Williamson, T. (2002) *The Transformation of Rural England: Farming and the Landscape 1700–1870.* Exeter: University of Exeter Press.

Williamson, T. (2003) *Shaping Medieval Landscapes: Settlement, Society, Environment.* Bollington: Windgather Press.

Zaluckyj. S. (2001) *Mercia: The Anglo Saxon Kingdom of Central England.* Almeley: Logaston.

Index

Page numbers in bold refer to illustrations.

The Peak District:
Landscapes
Through Time